AMERICA:
Standing Strong

An in-depth examination of the series of events Americans have endured in recent years and how we are

moving forward with solutions.

Robert J. Emery

"Time is like a river made up of the events that happen, and a violent stream; for as soon as a thing has been seen, it is carried away, and another comes in its place, and this will be carried away too."

—Marcus Aurelius Antoninus (121 AD – 180 AD)—
Last of the Roman rulers during the Pax Romana, which was an age of relative peace and stability.

Copyright © 2022 by Media Entertainment, Inc. All right reserved worldwide. No part of this publication may be replicated, redistributed, or given away in any form without the prior written consent of the author or publisher.

First Edition. Published June 2022 by Indies United Publishing House
Cover design by Vila Design – www.viladesing.net

Available E-Book, Paperback & Hardcover formats.

ISBN:
978-1-64456-445-5 [Hardback:]
978-1-64456-446-2 [Paperback]
978-1-64456-447-9 [ePub]
978-1-64456-486-8 [Mobi]
978-1-64456-471-4 [Audiobook]

Library of Congress Control Number: 9781644564455

Join Author Robert J. Emery online at:
http://www.robertjemeryauthor.com

INDIES UNITED PUBLISHING HOUSE, LLC
P.O. BOX 3071
QUINCY, IL 62305-3071
IndiesUnited.net

*To my wife Susanne for her endless support.
To family and friends for the same reason.*

*And to everyone on the planet who
wishes we could start all over again
and this time, we would get it right.*

Table of Contents

Introduction..1
Opening Salvo..9
Who Are We, Anyway?..............................14
Dictators:...35
International & Domestic Terrorism............52
America's Changing Demographics.............63
Anger & The Loss of Civility........................73
Whatever Happened to Common Sense?.....85
Racism in America......................................92
Guns In America..103
Our World's Deteriorating Environment....120
The 2020 Pandemic...................................136
Black Lives Matter:...................................154
The 2020 Election.....................................162
January 6, 2021..183
Conspiracy Theories & Misinformation.....205
Technology & Social Media......................225
Our Government.......................................244
The Constitution & American Democracy. 276
Closing Salvo..289
Lessons I Learned....................................292
Acknowledgments....................................317
ABOUT THE AUTHOR.............................319

Introduction

"Nothing vast enters the life of mortals without a curse."

—Sophocles—
c.496 BCE - 406 BCE
one of classical Athens's three great
tragic playwrights

We spend much of our lives trying to sort out the perplexities of life. We seek definitions. How did we get here? Why are we here? Does it make any sense? Can we make it better?

The good news is that when we muster our combined will, we meet challenges head-on, discovering new solutions and implementing them, for we are the masters of the planet. Like Mahatma Gandhi said, "The difference between what we do and what we are capable of doing would suffice to solve most of the world's problems."

And yet, these are trying times that test men's souls.

While running for president in 1920, Warren G. Harding spoke these words at a campaign stop in Boston: "America's present need is not heroics, but healing; not nostrums, but normalcy... The country does not require a revolution, but restoration; not agitation, but adjustment; not surgery, but serenity; not the dramatic, but the dispassionate; not experiment, but equipoise."

Mr. Harding's words ring true at a time when America and the world are experiencing more dark sunsets than bright sunrises. A wave of mental exhaustion has swept across all humankind, coalescing into one of the most tumultuous periods in recent memory. We seek normalcy, and it can't come fast enough. However, we cannot just wish all that has happened away. A wish, after all, is not a plan. It never is. We need, as Mr. Harding said, *restoration.*

So, with courage and conviction, we'll glance over our shoulders and examine the events and issues of the past six years, what went right and what went wrong, and how we can move forward.

I had the good fortune to read three books by investigative journalists Bob Woodward, Robert Costa, Michael Bender, and Evan Osnos. All are extraordinary documentation of the prior administration and the political turmoil that descended American politics. But there is another more urgent story that was not being written about that deals with the pain and suffering that Americans continue to endure beyond the political: the pandemic; the 2020 election; the Black Lives Matter movement; the January 6th attack on the Capital; the supply train problems; soaring food and gas prices; growing labor shortages; high rents causing thousands to go homeless; long lines at food banks; climate changes leading to increased heat waves, worse droughts, violent storms, and out of control fires. Our anxiety and frustration have left us feeling vulnerable.

There is a worldwide upheaval coming if it's not already here. This time, it feels different; this time, it feels dangerous. Where are the voices of common sense, reason, and compromise? There was a time when America's two-party system, for example, worked to advance American society despite philosophical differences. Today there is endless in-fighting and political posturing between the parties that do little to advance the lives of citizens. Enough already.

Research for this book began in mid-March of 2021 and continued for two months before the first word was written. Then, when completion was in sight in April of 2022, the medieval Russian invasion of Ukraine began. It was Syria all over again, with images of Ukrainian women, children, and the elderly crowding onto trains to escape the massacre and destruction. Able-bodied Ukrainian men remained behind to bravely fight for their country's independence as a democratically elected sovereign nation. The world held its collective breath, fearing Russia's invasion of Ukraine could escalate, sending the world into a world war.

A quote by scientist Albert Einstein reads like a dark prophecy. "I don't know with what weapons World War 3 will be fought, but World War 4 will be fought with sticks and stones." Mr. Einstein realized that humanity would create technology that, in time, would destroy most, if not all, of humanity.

In *Dr. Amishi P. Aha's eye-opening book, **Peak Mind**, there is a passage that sums up where America finds itself at this dangerously critical moment. "We are living in a time of uncertainty and change. Many of us are experiencing an atmosphere of stress and threat that constantly activates our minds' tendency to mentally travel to an alternate reality. The more stress and uncertainty we face, the more our minds journey to a desired or dystopic mental destination. Often, we are in fast-forward mode. We're trying to puzzle through all the uncertainty. We're mentally planning for events that aren't plannable. We're gaming our scenarios that may never come to pass."

STANDING STRONG

<u>Amishi P. Jha, PhD., is a professor of psychology and director of contemplative neuroscience at the University of Miami.</u> **"Peak Mind"** *<u>is available on</u>* **Amazon.com.**

As if the pain, suffering, and political divisiveness were not enough, there was an uptick of intrusive noise coming from an endless flow of misinformation and off-the-wall conspiracy theories. It was everywhere, inflicting confusion, fear, and consequences.

New York Times columnist *David Brooks wrote about this very issue in his contributing article for **TheAtlantic.com**: "Levels of trust in this country—in our institutions, politics, and one another—are in steep decline. And when social trust collapses, nations fail. Can we get it back before it's too late?... We had a chance, in crisis, to pull together as a nation and build trust. We did not. That has left us a broken, alienated society caught in a distrust doom loop."

<u>David Brooks is an Op-Ed columnist for The New York Times and a commentator on "PBS NewsHour" & NPR's "All Things Considered." To read the article, Google:</u> **America is Having a Moral Convulsion**.

Mr. Brook's words read like caution and

precaution. They're a call to arms, not with weapons or violence, but as a unified country to meet challenges head-on with honesty, truth, and facts and to roundly reject the voices of the wolves in sheep's clothing who would lead us in the wrong direction.

In the **Mahabharata**, one of the major Sanskrit epics of ancient India, the warrior Karna speaks the line: "I see it now—the world is swiftly passing."

And so it is, so it is, and we're running fast to catch up.

I am neither a scientist, scholar, nor philosopher. However, I am a concerned citizen of the world who remains curious, seeking answers from an everyman's perspective of the events in recent years that have adversely affected our society and possibly future generations.

I set out to gather and present the respected voices of investigative reporters, scholars, philosophers, scientists, medical professionals, and politicians across the political spectrum. They speak through the lens of truth and facts, not fiction, not conspiracy theories, and not misinformation. Included are thought-provoking quotes from past and present voices of reason. For those wishing to investigate further, sources are listed. We'll reexamine material most are familiar with, not to rehash what we already

STANDING STRONG

know but for those who may not or have yet to acknowledge.

There is no political bias intended here—the words and actions of those quoted or referred to speak for themselves. Right and wrong, truth and facts, morality and integrity, define every person's life. As the words carved in the original headquarters building of the CIA read, "And ye shall know the truth, and the truth shall make you free."

When award-winning documentarian Ken Burns sat for an interview with ***Variety.com*** to discuss his latest PBS documentary, "Benjamin Franklin," he spoke about how he and all Americans' were feelings. "I'm very anxious. I want my country to survive. I want to look back on all of this and go, 'Wow, that was tough, but we made it through' – just the way my parents and my grandparents talked to me about the depression. I want to have this in our rearview mirror, but I don't think that will happen for a while. It's going to take a concerted effort on the part of a lot of well-intentioned people not to stand by and just say, 'I don't agree with what is going on,' but to somehow get involved in the political process and shore up these institutions."

To read the article, Google: **Ken Burns' Urgent Warning: Why He's Scared for America's Future.**

AMERICA

Life is short; we only die once but live every day, so let us stay curious. Together, we forge ahead and seek answers to what brought us to this painful, dangerous moment in time and how we can stand strong as a nation and move forward as we always have.

"What's it all about?" Alfie was asked. A grim-faced Alfie replied, "I have no bloody idea, mate."

This book was completed in April 2022, leaving many issues unresolved and ongoing. So, read on, dear citizens of the world, and always remain curious. It's a short book, don't skip any pages. We have a few chapters to plow through before we get to the hard stuff.

—The Author—

Opening Salvo

Close your eyes and keep them closed. Now imagine your defying gravity and floating freely further and further up into the sky, passing through thick clouds and the Kármán line, the boundary between Earth's atmosphere and the blackness of outer space. Now open your eyes and peer down. What do you see?

There, off in the far distance of space, Mother Earth sits like a polished jewel. Large swatches of green, brown, and blue dot the surface where the planet is in daylight, and intricate artistic swirls of scattered clouds cover portions of the sky. Where the sun has set, the earth is shining with a dazzling display of lights. At that moment, no words can describe your emotions. It is a heart-stopping sight that only a brave group of astronauts have been privileged to witness.

You hear yourself say low, "Holy Mother of God!"

AMERICA

"It suddenly struck me that that tiny pea, pretty and blue, was the Earth. I put up my thumb and shut one eye, and my thumb blotted out the planet Earth. It didn't feel like a giant. I felt very, very small."

—Neil Armstrong—
(1930 – 2012)
The first person to walk on the Moon

How did this planet that Astronaut Armstrong gazed upon come to be, and how did we come to be the masters of it? Those are questions we'd all like to see answered, but we may never know.

"All things are subject to interpretation whichever interpretation prevails at a given time is a function of power and not truth."

—Friedrich Nietzsche—
(1844 – 1900)
German philosopher, cultural critic, composer, poet, writer

STANDING STRONG

William Goldman (1931-2018), an award-winning novelist, playwright, and screenwriter, coined three words that best describe our never-ending but often unsuccessful quest for knowledge and truth when he said, "Nobody knows anything." Those three insightful words remain accurate today when applied like a surgeon's scalpel across the human spectrum. We are, after all, human and, by definition, fallible, influenced by our emotions, egos, prejudices, and biases. Every day is a crap shoot of endless ideas, opinions, arguments, and controversies.

"The only true wisdom is in knowing you know nothing."

—Socrates—
(470 BC – 399 BC)
Greek philosopher from Athens who is credited as a founder of Western philosophy

Since no one person has all the answers, it takes a "village" to find solutions to pressing world issues. That is if we can stop our arguing, hatred of others, and efforts to convince others that our way is better and they should think, believe, and act as we do.

AMERICA

If one day we can move beyond these sophomoric and self-destructive traits and get on with a unified effort to work on behalf of all humanity, we just might begin making meaningful progress.

"Knowledge is invariably a matter of degree: you cannot put your finger upon even the simplest datum and say this, we know."

—*T. S. Eliot*—
(1888 – 1965)
Poet, essayist, publisher, playwright, literary critic, & editor

In the 1997 national bestselling book, ***The Fourth Turning***, co-author *Neil Howe offered hope for the future: "To be clear, the road ahead for America will be rough. But I take comfort in the idea that history cycles back and that the past offers us a guide to what we can expect in the future. Like Nature's four seasons, the cycles of history follow a natural rhythm or pattern."

<u>Neil Howe is an American author and consultant known for his work with William Strauss on social generations regarding a theorized generational cycle in American history.</u>
"The Fourth Turning" *is available on **Amazon.com.***

STANDING STRONG

We should add to Mr. Howe's statement that although everything changes, nothing changes. Is it because we pay so little attention to history's lessons? Like the caged hamster racing around its wheel, we return to the same starting point generation after generation. Why? The past should be our guide to what works and what does not. If we don't heed the mistakes of the past, we fail to pay it forward to future generations. Instead, we burden them with the crumbs we leave behind, and the cycle begins again.

> *"I believe our future depends on how well we know this Cosmos in which we float like a mote of dust in the morning sky."*

—*Carl Sagan*—
(1934 – 1996)
Astronomer, planetary scientist, cosmologist, astrophysicist, astrobiologist, author, and science communicator

AMERICA

<u>Who Are We, Anyway?</u>

> *"No society has been able to abolish human sadness, no political system can deliver us from the pain of living, from our fear of death, our thirst for the absolute. It is the human condition that directs the social condition, not vice versa."*
>
> **—*Eugene Ionesco*—**
> (1909 – 1994)
> A Romanian-French playwright who was one of the foremost figures of the French avant-garde theatre in the 20th century

Let's begin with this explanation from **Wikipedia**: "The human condition is all of the characteristics and key events that compose the essentials of human existence, including birth, growth, emotion, aspiration, conflict, and mortality. This is an extensive topic that has been and continues to be pondered and analyzed from many perspectives, including anthropology, art, biology, history, literature, philosophy, psychology, and religion.

In short, we're still trying to figure out who we are. If anyone tells you they know the answer, curl your lips in a slightly cynical grin, refer to William Goldman's three words of wisdom, and beat a hasty retreat.

Britannica.com comes closer to a realistic answer: "Are humans essentially kind, sensible, good-natured creatures? Or are we, deep down, wired to be bad, blinkered, idle, vain, vengeful, and selfish?" asks Britannica. "There are no easy answers, and there's clearly a lot of variation between individuals, but here we shine some evidence-based light on the matter through 10 dispiriting findings that reveal the darker and less impressive aspects of human nature: We view minorities and the vulnerable as less than human; We experience Schadenfreude (pleasure at another person's distress) by the age of four; We believe in karma – assuming that the downtrodden of the world deserve their fate; We are blinkered and dogmatic; We would rather electrocute ourselves than spend time in our thoughts; We are vain and overconfident; We are moral hypocrites; We are all potential trolls; We favor ineffective leaders with psychopathic traits; We are sexually attracted to people with dark personality traits."

To read the Britannica article, Google: ***The bad news on human nature, in 10 findings from psychology.***

That's a rather severe condemnation of humanity. But the emotions Britannica boldly suggests are genuine for everyone. We are the product of our bloodline, upbringing, environment, culture, and education, and depending on how we are affected by each, they can trigger the more vicious side of our personality characteristics. Hopefully, not too often.

The majority of us Homo sapiens are generous, cooperative, social, and want the best for ourselves and others. However, in a complicated and dangerous world, it is often difficult to practice our positive traits in the face of adversity. In recent years, we've endured adversities ad nauseam.

Many Americans report high stress due to the hyper-polarized political atmosphere, financial concerns, inflation, the COVID-19 pandemic, and the Russian invasion of Ukraine. "The number of people who say they're significantly stressed about these most recent events is stunning relative to what we've seen since we began the survey in 2007," Arthur C. Evans Jr., Ph.D., and CEO of the American Phycological Association said in a statement: "Americans have been doing their best to persevere over these past two tumultuous years, but these data suggest that we're now reaching unprecedented stress levels that will challenge our coping ability," he said.

To read the article, Google: ***Most Americans Report Overwhelming Stress Levels: Poll***

We have lived through a period of confusion, fear, anger, and painful consequences that have left many in a mental state of denial, making us susceptible to the crackpots and wolves in sheep's clothing pushing conspiracy theories and misinformation. We've heard them all, but some are worth repeating: China created the pandemic to destroy our economy. Why are we poisoning ourselves with these unproven and dangerous vaccines and wearing these ridiculous facemasks? And everyone knows climate change is a hoax perpetrated by progressives. The supply chain slowdown and rising inflation are also a hoax. It's big business ripping us off for higher profits. Yeah, the 2020 election was rigged for sure. The January 6 invasion of the U.S Capital was patriots exercising their rights. The threat of World War 3 is a government scare tactic to keep us in line. Otherwise, everything is okay; everything is just fine. The real world can't touch us as long as we remain comfortably curled in the fetal position in our private bubble of reality, blocking out the truth, facts, and consequences. But hey, everything is okay; everything is just fine.

Everything is *not* okay; everything is *not* just fine.

We may not have had control over some of what happened, but we are responsible for our responses, actions, or inactions that added fuel to the fire.

Leading Astrophysicist *Adam Frank explores what daily life is like for most of us in his article, **"The Mystery of Life Cannot Be Solved by Science,"** for ***BigThink.com***. Mr. Frank writes that reductionism—the practice of simplifying a complex idea, issue, or condition—may be a way to explain our universe. Still, it cannot replace our personal experiences, nor does it answer the question of who we are. Frank writes, "Every morning you emerge from sleep, open your eyes, and find that... yup... you are still here. Another day on the planet—breathing, eating, and working so you can keep breathing, eating, and working. You're trying to hold it all together while having a little fun." Mr. Frank says. "Then, after about 16 hours, you will drop back into bed with one day less left in your life inventory, knowing you have to repeat the whole effort tomorrow. This is the reality, in one form or another, for you, me, and every other human being on the planet. It has also been the reality, in one form or another, for human beings since we emerged as a separate species. All in all, it seems pretty weird. What's it all for? Is there a mystery to life?"

Astrophysicist Adam Frank is a self-described "evangelist of science," committed to showing others the beauty and power of science. To read the article, Google: **The mystery of life cannot be solved by science.**

Most would relate to another interpretation that strikes closer to our reality.

> *"My mom always said life was like a box of chocolates. You never know what you're gonna get."*

—*Forest Gump*—

Actor Tom Hanks spoke those iconic words in the 1994 motion picture *Forrest Gump*. There are few sentences in the English language that describe life more veraciously. Like a toss of the dice, one day we roll a 7 or

11, and we win; the next, a 2, 3, or 12, and we lose. Bummer! Let's roll those dice again.

Eleanor Roosevelt (1884-1962), First Lady of the United States, weighed in on the subject during her husband, President Franklin D. Roosevelt's Presidency: "In the long run, we shape our lives, and we shape ourselves. The process never ends until we die. And the choices we make are ultimately our own responsibility."

Our choices are ultimately our own, and those choices place responsibility squarely on us, the most intelligent species on the planet. Today's decisions determine the road we travel tomorrow and, together, the road humanity travels.

Yes, it's complicated; it always is.

"Everything may be labeled, but everybody is not."

—Edith Wharton—
(1862 – 1937)
American novelist, short story writer, and designer.
The above quote is from her novel, "The Age of Innocence," Published in 1920.

Let's roll this film back to the beginning, back to launch day, our birth. It depends on who provided our early guidance to influence our values and sense of right and wrong from that day on. St. Ignatius Loyal, the founder of the Jesuit Brotherhood, put it this way: "Give me a child 'till he is seven years old, and I will show you the man."

There's no argument there; unfortunately, not everyone who gets to procreate is created equal. If a child's first seven years are mishandled, those years are complex—often impossible—to recover.

When navigating the trenches of Google, I came across this discerning comment on **Quora.com** from a lady named ***Kate,*** who, as a parent, understood that she bore responsibility for the values her children would carry to adulthood but was also aware that outside influences could affect them as adults.

"Way back when I had not been teaching long... when I was young, childless and somewhat ignorant... I came to the conclusion that children are a product of their parents. I didn't just mean that in a purely biological sense, either. I meant it in a 'whoa, mamma; we've created a monster' kind of way. Sure, other things influence a child as they grow up, but they are minor when compared to the influence a parent has on the sort of person their kids turn out to be. Now, some years later, with almost eight years of parenthood under my belt, I am not so sure if I believe that notion quite so wholeheartedly. Perhaps it is because, as a parent, that is a darn scary idea to contemplate. We, The Father Figure and I, what we say, how we do things, who we are, just us, we are responsible for the kind of adults our children will become. Or perhaps it is because I am older and wiser and, perhaps, I can see now that as a child grows, the influence that I, as a parent, have over them lessens. But does that giving way to outside influences ever really negate the powerful influence of a parent?"

We do the best we can, Kate, and we hope we did it right.

*Check out Kate's fun blog, Google: **Picklebums**.

> *"The individual has always had to struggle to keep from being overwhelmed by the tribe. If you try it, you will be lonely often and sometimes frightened. But no price is too high to pay for the privilege of owning yourself."*
>
> **—Friedrich Nietzsche—**
> (1844 – 1900)
> German philosopher, cultural critic, composer, poet, and writer

Our initial tribe consists of our parents, relatives, and friends. They protect and encourage us and are there for us in times of need. What would we do without them guiding us? Hold on, not so fast; depending on the tribe one is born to, there's a dark side to this story.

An excerpt from *Elizabeth A. Segal's piece in ***PhycologyToday.com*** supports Nietzsche's quote that others influence us within our tribes: "... The worst type of tribalism is groups aligned to destroy other groups, such as through ethnic cleansing and genocide," Ms. Segal said. "Today in our political world, we have 'bad tribalism.' Bad tribalism is a group identity that fosters the bullying and scapegoating of others, not like you. Bad tribalism joins people out of anger, jealousy, and spite, not for collective well-being. The unfortunate irony is that bad tribalism is easy to provoke but not healthy to maintain," Segal said.

Elizabeth A. Segal, Ph.D., is a professor in the School of Social Work at Arizona State University. To read the article, Google: **When Tribalism Goes Bad.*

AMERICA

"No man's life can be encompassed in one telling. There is no way to give each year its allotted weight, to include each event, each person who helped to shape a lifetime. What can be done is to be faithful in spirit to the record and try to find one's way to the heart of the man."

—*Mahatma Gandhi*—
(1869 – 1948)
Indian lawyer, anti-colonial nationalist, and political an ethicist who led the successful campaign for India's independence from British rule.

Gandhi's wisdom should serve as a roadmap to all of us on how to respect others as we would like others to respect us in return. That's not always easy to do in a world of good and evil, but we are obligated to try, and try we do.

STANDING STRONG

"When I look up at the night sky, and I know that, yes, we are part of this Universe, we are in this Universe, but perhaps more important than both of those acts are that the Universe is in us. When I reflect on that fact, I look up — many people feel small because they're small, and the Universe is big, but I feel big because my atoms came from those stars."

—*Neil deGrasse Tyson*—
American Astrophysicist

As we enter the third and final act of our lives, we peer over our shoulders more and more at the past, examining where we've been, what we may or may not have accomplished, and those we shared our lives with. The question lingers: Besides being a non-stop slam-bang rollercoaster ride from start to finish, did our life have meaning?

AMERICA

"In my life, I have found two things of priceless worth— learning and loving. Nothing else —not name, not power, not achievement for its own sake – can possibly have the same lasting value. or when your life is over, if you can say 'I have learned, and I have loved,' you will also be able to say... I have been happy."

—*Arthur C. Clarke*—
(1917 – 2008)
Science-fiction writer, co-author of 2001: A Space Odyssey, one of the most influential films of all time.

No matter what challenges we face, we humans never lose our passion, compassion, enthusiasm, creativity, innovation, and the spark to seek better lives for ourselves, our families, and others. That much we know; that's what keeps us going. The human spirit propels us forward in an extraordinarily complicated, fast-moving world.

STANDING STRONG

"March on. Do not tarry. To go forward is to move toward perfection. March on, and fear not the thorns or the sharp stones on life's path."

—*Khalil Gibran*—
(1883-1931)
Lebanese-American writer, poet and visual artist & philosopher

No discussion of who we are would be complete without our insane propensity to go to war with one another. Our capacity to hate others is played out on battlefields, where human life is disposable. What in the world are we thinking? How does any war advance humanity? There are even humanitarian rules of war as written by the Geneva Conventions and the International Committee of the Red Cross. As the presupposed most intelligent living creature on the planet, how can we be so ignorant to believe a set of rules have any meaning in the heat of battle? Do these rules sanction wars as long as the rules are followed? Insane.

If you visit Washington, D.C., see the memorials on the National Mall that pay tribute to past wars and the men and women who bravely served in them. You cannot help but stand and gaze upon these monuments and wonder if, one day in the future, another memorial will be erected in memory of yet another insane war.

The late Madeleine Jana Korbel Albright, born Marie Jana Korbelová on May 15, 1937, immigrated to the United States with her family in 1948 from Communist Czechoslovakia. She graduated from Wesley College and went on to earn a Ph.D. from Columbia University, and she served as the 64th United States secretary of state, the first woman to hold that post. Before her death in 2022, Ms. Albright wrote about making the most out of life in her memoir. She passes on to us an essential lesson in hope. Here is an excerpt of her thoughts from ***"Hell and Other Destinations: A 21st Century Memoir."***

"No matter how smart we are, we can allow sorrows and grievances to overwhelm us, or we can respond positively to setbacks caused by our misjudgments or by forces beyond our control. This choice has rarely been starker than in the past two years. As individuals, we have had to adapt to the shock of unpleasant and unexpected circumstances. Collectively, we have had to bounce back from the pandemic and from doubts about our willingness to pursue social justice, our power to make self-government succeed, and our capacity to prevent advanced technology from causing more harm than good. Worldwide, we have undergone a period of trial that has changed us in ways not yet fully revealed. Our future leaders will have to be bold and resourceful, and so, each in our own way, will we. I have a measure of sympathy but little patience for those who despair of that possibility. There is no shortage of worthwhile work to be done and no surplus of seasons in which to achieve our goals. So let us buckle up our boots, grab a cane if we need one, and march on."

*Ms. Albright's book "**Hell and Other Destinations: A 21st Century Memoir**" is available on **Amazon.com***

"The proper function of man is to live, not to exist. I shall not waste my days trying to prolong them. I shall use my time."

—*Jack London*—
(1876 -1916)
American novelist, journalist, & social activist. A pioneer of commercial fiction and American magazines

AMERICA

An Internet search credited the following poem to "Anonymous." Apologies to the younger generations who may not associate with many of the names. Feel free to replace them with those from your generation. If you read it carefully, the message will remain the same; one day, old and frail, all we will have left is our memories. Hopefully, most are good ones.

"Long ago and far away, in a land that time forgot, before the days of Dylan, or the dawn of Camelot, there lived a race of innocents, and they were you and me. Ike (Eisenhower) was in the White House in that land where we were born, where navels were for oranges, and Peyton Place was porn. We longed for love and romance, and waited for our Prince. Eddie Fisher married Liz Taylor, and no one's seen him since. We danced to 'Little Darlin,' and sang to 'Stagger Lee' and cried for Buddy Holly in the Land That Made Me, Me. Only girls wore earrings then, and three was one too many, and only boys wore flat-top cuts, except for Jean McKinney. And only in our wildest dreams did we expect to see a boy named George with Lipstick in the Land That Made Me, Me. We fell for Frankie Avalon, Annette was oh, so nice, and when they made a movie, they never made it twice. We didn't have a Star Trek Five, or Psycho

STANDING STRONG

Two and Three, or Rocky-Rambo Twenty in the Land That Made Me, Me. Miss Kitty had a heart of gold, and Chester had a limp, and Reagan was a Democrat whose co-star was a chimp. We had a Mr. Wizard, but not a Mr. T, and Oprah couldn't talk yet, in the Land That Made Me, Me. We had our share of heroes; we never thought they'd go, at least not Bobby Darin or Marilyn Monroe. For youth was still eternal, and life was yet to be, and Elvis was forever in the Land That Made Me, Me. We'd never seen the rock band that was Grateful to be Dead, and Airplanes weren't named Jefferson, and Zeppelins were not Led. And Beatles lived in gardens then, and Monkeys lived in trees, Madonna was Mary in the Land That Made Me, Me. We'd never heard of microwaves or telephones in cars, and babies might be bottle-fed, but they were not grown in jars. And pumping iron got wrinkles out, and 'gay' meant fancy-free, and dorms were never co-Ed in the Land That Made Me, Me. We hadn't seen enough of jets to talk about the lag, and microchips were what was left at the bottom of the bag. And hardware was a box of nails, and bytes came from a flea, and rocket ships were fiction in the Land That Made Me, Me. T-Birds came with portholes, and side shows came with freaks, and bathing suits came big enough to cover both your cheeks. And Coke came just

AMERICA

in bottles and skirts below the knee, and Castro came to power near the Land That Made Me, Me. We had no Crest with Fluoride; we had no Hill Street Blues; we had no patterned pantyhose or Lipton herbal tea. Or prime-time ads for those dysfunctions in the Land That Made Me, Me. There were no golden arches, no Perrier to chill, and fish were not called Wanda, and cats were not called Bill. And middle-aged was 35 and old was forty-three, and ancient were our parents in the Land That Made Me, Me. But all things have a season, or so we've heard them say, and now instead of Maybelline, we swear by Retin-A. They send us invitations to join AARP; we've come a long way, baby, from the Land That Made Me, Me. So now we face a brave new world in slightly larger jeans and wonder why they're using smaller print in magazines. And we tell our children's children of the way it used to be, long ago and far away in the Land That Made Me, Me."

<u>*To view the poem with photos and narration, Google:*</u>
<u>The Land That Made Me, Me.</u>

There you have it; that's who we are, or at least who we think we are. When we are gone from this Earth, we will only be remembered by what we left behind, worth remembering by those we left behind. Otherwise, we are soon forgotten, and the world goes on.

STANDING STRONG

The final word goes to the brilliant Steve Jobs, who departed this earth way too early. Forbes Magazine wrote of him: "Steve was and remains a role model for struggling entrepreneurs, ousted business leaders, college drop-outs, adoptees, and disease-fighting people who could relate to his journey."

"Our time is limited, so don't waste it living someone else's life."

—Steve Jobs—
(1955 -2011)
American business magnate, industrial designer, investor and media proprietor

AMERICA

There are world events that we as individuals have no control over, although they may affect us somehow. Three of them are Dictators, International and Domestic Terrorism, and America's Changing Demographics.

This is where we begin our journey, a journey that demands our attention, expertise, creativity, patience, and above all, unified common-sense decisions to deal with a fast-changing globally-connected world.

Stay with me; it gets messier as we proceed.

Dictators: Destroyers of Societies

"Those who deny freedom to others deserve it not for themselves; and, under a just God, cannot retain it.

—Abraham Lincoln—
(1809 – 1865)
16th president of the United States

Throughout human history, dictators have been humanity's worst nightmare.

For example, Julius Caesar, Emperor of the Roman Empire, had become obsessed with his self-importance. He was stabbed to death in Rome's Senate House on the ides of March in 44 B.C. by men who wanted to retain the Roman Republic and were convinced that Caesar had to be stopped.

AMERICA

"Our tyrant deserved to die. Here was a man who wanted to be king of the Roman people and master of the whole world. Those who agree with an ambition like this must also accept the destruction of existing laws and freedoms. It is not right or fair to want to be king in a state that used to be free and ought to be free today."

—Gaius Matius—
(Born 100 BC, Rome, Italy)
Roman general, politician, and statesman

"They thought they were liberating Rome, but instead, they put the nail in the coffin of the free republic." Author Barry Strauss wrote in ***Ten Caesars: Roman Emperors from Augustus to Constantine***.

For Roman history buffs like myself, author Strauss' book makes for fascinating reading.

<u>Barry Strauss' book **"Ten Caesars: Roman Emperors from Augustus to Constantine"** is available on Amazon.com.</u>

STANDING STRONG

"Make the lie big. Make it simple. Keep saying it, and eventually, people will believe it."

—Adolf Hitler—
(1889 – 1945)
Austrian-born German politician &
Dictator of Germany

The late 20th Century witnessed a rise in authoritarian regimes. Some remain in power today; others are long gone. They all have one thing in common; they leave behind a country in ruin, whether they die or are ousted. In recent history, the list of men with evil intentions includes Adolf Hitler-Germany, Vladimir Lenin-Soviet Union, Joseph Stalin-Soviet Union, Benito Mussolini-Italy, Francisco Franco-Spain, Josip Tito-Yugoslavia, Nicolas Maduro-Venezuela, Vladimir Putin-Russia, Recep Tayyip Erdogan-Turkey, Daniel Ortega-Nicaragua.

Every one of them was and is a vile, self-serving, ego-driven tyrant, men who crave absolute power with zero regards for the well-being of the people they govern.

AMERICA

"One does not establish a dictatorship in order to safeguard a revolution; one makes a revolution in order to establish a dictatorship."

—George Orwell—
(1903 -1950)
Eric Arthur Blair, pen name George Orwell, an English novelist, essayist, journalist, and critic

If you watch the ANCHD cable channel, you will learn the entire history of what Hitler and his regime did to the Jews. At least one-episode documents allied troops entering German concentration camps where millions of Jews were put to death. Not long after the war ended, psychologists began to examine why so many German citizens, who certainly had to know what was going on, stood by the atrocities and remained loyal to a cruel leader and his Nazi Party. The five reasons they found were: Power of Authority; Power of Limited Information; Power of Gradually Increasing Demands; Power of Avoiding Personal Responsibility; the Power of Fear.

That last one—fear—works every time, even today. Sound familiar?

On ***PsychologyToday.com.***, *Diane E.

Dreher writes: "When we react out of fear, we're not using our thought processes to analyze the situation but rather responding automatically to a supposed threat." Dreher said. "When authoritarian leaders, or those who show such tendencies, keep us fearful and emotionally off-balance, repeated stress can become underlying anxiety, more readily triggering us into new fear reactions. With our ability to think compromised, our fears can make us more easily manipulated by authoritarian leaders."

Dreher confirms what we have come to know; autocratic-leaning leaders are narcissistic, constantly need their ego's stroked, possess antisocial personality disorder traits, lack empathy for others, have a driving need for absolute power, are indifferent to conventional laws or rules or morality, regularly feed the public lies and propaganda, and are quick to dowl out retribution to anyone disloyal to them. The list should be enough to one day say *never again* and join forces to stop would-be dictators before they can rise to power.

*Diane Dreher, Ph.D., is an award-winning university professor and positive psychology researcher and the author of the best-selling **"Tao of Inner Peace"** available on Amazon.com*
To read the article, Google: **Why Do People Follow Authoritarian Leaders?**

AMERICA

> *"Absolute power turns its possessors not into God but an anti-God. For God turned clay into men, while the absolute despot turns men into clay."*
>
> **—Eric Hoffer—**
> (1902 – 1983)
> American moral and social philosopher

In an episode of the **HistoryExtra** podcast, historian *Frank Dikötter, author of **How to Be a Dictator**, wrote: "I believe that there are two main instruments that dictators use – one is terror and the other one is image. Now the terror, we know – the concentration camps; the secret police; the knock-on-the-door in the middle of the night; the atrocious crimes against humanity – but I think image, in particular, the 'cult of personality, we tend to overlook a bit – even though if you look at the 20th century, literally hundreds of millions of people cheered their own dictators, even as they were led down the road to serve them."

Make of that what you will.

*Frank Dikötter's book, **"How to Be a Dictator,"** is available on **Amazon.com**.

STANDING STRONG

"Where justice is denied, where poverty is enforced, where ignorance prevails, and where any one class is made to feel that society is an organized conspiracy to oppress, rob, and degrade them; neither persons nor property will be safe."

—*Frederick Douglass*—
(1818-1895)
Social reformer, abolitionist, orator, writer, & statesman

Tyrants succeed because they either have the backing of the people or, once in power, they rig the system in their favor to remain in power. And yet, history demonstrates that those who back an authoritarian leader eventually realize their tyrant's craving for absolute power and authority over them is more important than the riches these tyrants accumulate.

In her article in ***PsychologyToday.com***, Jean Kim M.D. writes: "While people often discuss the history of malignant behavior and records of sadism and the horrific aftermath of these tyrants, what is discussed less often is that these leaders do not and cannot rise in a vacuum; they come to power on the backs of the masses, they ultimately disdain and discard at will. It's the people who follow these bully dictator types that we need to examine and reflect on as well; why do people worship and enable these leaders? What is it in human nature that makes us vulnerable to this repeated cycle of cruelty and danger?"

<u>Dr. Jean Kim is a surgeon-scientist & Associate Professor of Otolaryngology-Head & Neck Surgery at Johns Hopkins University School of Medicine. To read the article, Google:</u> **Why Do People Follow Tyrants?**

Are the people who support those with authoritarian tendencies educated enough to recognize the evil behind the mask and stop them in their tracks? Once the autocrat attains power, those in official positions who serve them are often afraid to speak for fear of retribution. Or, like the Generals and Oligarchs in Russia, they are handsomely rewarded for their loyalty.

> *"Do you know what happens with people who cannot govern themselves? That's right. Others come in to govern for them."*

—*Cormac McCarthy*—
Prolific American writer well known for graphic depictions of violence and unique writing style.

STANDING STRONG

Not every country is labeled a true dictatorship. Today there are countries whose citizens live and suffer in less than a democracy while their leadership thrives.

Here is a list of those currently labeled as "Not Free" assembled by ***FreedomHouse.org***. Afghanistan; Algeria–Angola; Azerbaijan; Bahrain; Belarus; Brunei; Burundi; Cambodia; –Cameroon; Central African Republic; Chad; China; Congo; Dem. Rep. of –Congo; Rep of (Brazzaville); Cuba; Djibouti; Egypt; Equatorial Guinea; Eritrea; –Ethiopia; Gabon; Iran; Iraq; Kazakhstan; Laos; Libya; Myanmar; Nicaragua; –North Korea; Oman; Qatar; Russia; Rwanda; Saudi Arabia; Somalia; South Sudan; Sudan; Swaziland (Eswatini); Syria; Tajikistan; Turkey; Turkmenistan; Uganda; United Arab Emirates; Uzbekistan; Venezuela; Vietnam; Western Sahara; Yemen.

It is a shameful list in the year 2022.

To read the article, Google: **Democracy in Retreat.**

AMERICA

"Dictatorships naturally arise out of democracy, and the most aggravated form of tyranny and slavery out of the most extreme liberty."

—*Plato*—

(Born & died in Athens, Greece)
Greek philosopher and founder of the Platonist school of thought and the Academy, the first institution of higher learning in the Western world

This riveting must-read article in **TheAtlantic.com, *The Bad Guys Are Winning*,** is from *Anne Applebaum. "If the 20th century was the story of slow, uneven progress toward the victory of liberal democracy over other ideologies—communism, fascism, virulent nationalism—the 21st century is, so far, a story of the reverse." She wrote: "If Americans, together with our allies, fail to fight the habits and practices of autocracy abroad, we will encounter them at home; indeed, they are already here. If Americans don't help to hold murderous regimes to account, those regimes will retain their sense of impunity. They will continue to steal, blackmail, torture, and intimidate inside their countries—and ours."

STANDING STRONG

*<u>Anne Applebaum is a staff writer at The Atlantic, a fellow at the SNF Agora Institute at Johns Hopkins University, and the author of **"Twilight of Democracy: The Seductive Lure of Authoritarianism,"** available at **Amazon.com**. The article **"The Bad Guys Are Winning"** is available at **TheAtlantic.com**.</u>

We should heed Ms. Applebaum's warning. It can happen in any country; it can happen here. There has been saber-rattling within a segment of American society, extolling the benefits of an autocratic government. Who are these people, who are behind them, what is the source of their funding, and for what end purpose?

It can happen in any country.

> *"Experience hath shown that even under the best forms of government, those entrusted with power have, in time, and by slow operations perverted it into tyranny."*

—*Thomas Jefferson*—
(1743 – 1826)
3rd President of the United States

How do would-be tyrants destroy democracies? *Larry Diamond explains.

"The death of democracy is now typically administered in a thousand cuts. In one country after another, elected leaders have gradually attacked the deep tissues of democracy—the independence of the courts, the business community, the media, civil society, universities, and sensitive state institutions like the civil service, the intelligence agencies, and the police."

*<u>Larry Diamond is an American political sociologist and leading contemporary scholar in democracy studies and one of the world's foremost scholars on democracy. To read the article, Google: **Our Democracy is in Danger.**</u>*

America's Founding Fathers were concerned enough about tyranny to have fashioned a system of government that would, hopefully, impede it. Alexander Hamilton raised a red flag against the likes of "Catiline or Caesar," foxes camouflaged in sheep's clothing, in their attempts to rise to absolute power. We shrug and ignore them at our own risk.

> *"There are men running Governments who shouldn't be allowed to play with matches."*
>
> **—Will Rogers—**
> (1879 – 1935)
> Actor, humorist, newspaper columnist, social commentator

Except for whatever history is still being taught in schools, our children remain in the

STANDING STRONG

dark about the wars and skirmishes of the past. Here for the record, is a list of battles that massacred humans on a mass scale. The Boer War, 1899-1902; 1st World War, 1914-1918; Russian Civil War, 1917-1922; 3rd Afghan War, 1919; Irish War of Independence, 1919-1921; Irish Civil War, 1922-1923; Spanish Civil War, 1936-1939; Arab Revolt in Palestine, 1936-1939: 2nd World War, 1939-1945; Jewish insurgency in Mandatory Palestine, 1944-1948; Partition of India, 1947; Israeli-Palestinian Conflict, 1948 onwards; Malayan Emergency, 1948-1960; Yangtze Incident, 1949; Korean War, 1950-1953; Kenya Emergency, 19521960; Cyprus Emergency, 1955-1959; Vietnam War, 1955-1975; Suez Crisis, 1956; Brunei Revolt, 1962-1963; Indonesian Confrontation, 1963-1966; Aden Emergency, 1963-1967; The Troubles (Northern Ireland conflict), 1968-1998; Falkland Islands War, 1982; Gulf War, 1990-1991; Sierra Leone Civil War, 1991-2002; Bosnia War, 1992-1995; Kosovo War, 1998-1999; War in Afghanistan, 2001-2011; Iraq War, 2003-2011; Libya Conflict, 2011-present; Syria Conflict, 2011-present; Yemen Conflict, 2014-present; Global Coalition to Defeat ISIS, 2014-present.

If the above list is not an unforgivable and shameful document of human behavior and suffering, nothing is.

AMERICA

At 6:15 AM on February 25th, 2022, we all watched in horror on the news that humanity's worst nightmare began as Russian dictator, Vladimir Putin, directed his military forces to invade Ukraine. For the younger generations, they are witnessing their first look at war and its utter destruction of lives and property. For those old enough to recall past battles, it is a painful reminder of the brutality and horrors of war.

As he was dying at the end of the motion picture ***Apocalypse Now***, Marlon Brando whispered, "Oh, the horror, the horror."

> *"Education isn't memorizing that Hitler killed 6 million Jews. Education is understanding how millions of ordinary Germans were convinced that it was required. Real education is learning how to spot the signs of history repeating itself. We must never forget what hate does to us."*

—*George#VotesBlueAlways*—
@Numbers28Progressive, engineer, grandpa, polyglot, world traveler & Loves humans

STANDING STRONG

The news that former and current American high-level officials and others in influential public positions have openly and ignorantly expressed support for Putin's illegal invasion of Ukraine should make all Americans angry. That tells us all we need to know about their zealous political ambitions. They are power-hungry imposters masquerading as patriots, and we must not allow ourselves to be fooled. Americans should be asking who, what, where, why, and what purpose?

> *"We must especially beware of that small group of selfish men who would clip the wings of the American Eagle in order to feather their own nests."*
>
> **—*Franklin D. Roosevelt*—**
> (1933 – 1945)
> 32nd President of the United States

Not only are President Roosevelt's words of caution worth our attention, but this would be as good a time to remind ourselves that it is a few minutes to midnight on the Doomsday Clock. We have enough problems facing us.

AMERICA

A call to action. What can we do to stop would-be dictators? We can remain vigilant by making every effort to learn all we can about a candidate before supporting them at the federal or state level. Many candidates with vainglorious ambitions conflict with American values. Place ideology and political party affiliation aside long enough to recognize and reject the wolves in sheep's clothing. That much we can do, that much we must do to preserve a democracy built on the backs of those who came before us and who made America one of the world's most significant bastions of freedom. If we fail to take these simple steps, we could awaken to find ourselves living under... *fill in the rest.*

The **Consequences** of living under authoritarian leaders.

>*Dictators display a blatant disregard for human life.
>*Their goal is to advance themselves, not those they govern.
>*They restrict the right of citizens & censures the press and the Internet.
>*They misuse their power at the expense of citizens.
>*Their rule leads to poor health,

education systems, and poverty.
*Can lead to internal and external wars.
*They cause repression, human rights abuses, and turmoil.
*Despots advance their support among the elite through corrupt practices.
*They limit international relations with other countries.
*Dictators are narcissistic and ego-driven and are not in touch with reality.

The final word goes to the brilliant scientist Albert Einstein. His words apply to everyone living in and cherishing a true democracy.

"The world will not be destroyed by those who do evil, but by those who watch without them doing anything."

—*Albert Einstein*—
(1878 – 1955)
German-born theoretical physicist

AMERICA

International & Domestic Terrorism

"Every leader, and every regime, and every movement, and every organization that steps across the line of terrorism must be banished from the discourse of civilized human life."

—*Alan Lee Keyes*—
Conservative political activist, pundit, author, and former ambassador

Although this section deals primarily with domestic terrorism in America, we must first understand who terrorists are, whether they be international or domestic. What motivates them? Why do they have no empathy for the pain and suffering they inflict on their victims to achieve their illicit end goals?

Terrorists were first described as a person or a group seeking to violently overturn constituted forms and institutions of society and government without establishing another system of order to replace the existing structure they wanted so badly to destroy. Socialists, fascists, anarchists—whatever name they fall under—terrorists are all the same carrying out their vicious attacks with warped ideologies or personal grievances. In the words of theoretical physicist Edward teller, "Despair and fanaticism are only differing manifestations of evil."

> *"Terrorism has become the systematic weapon of a war that knows no borders or seldom has a face."*
>
> **—*Jacques Chirac*—**
> (1932 – 2019)
> Former President of France - previously Prime Minister of France - Mayor of Paris

It might surprise that all acts of terrorism don't fall within standard definitions, especially when treating high-ranking officials in the international community. Not many will recall that by 1996, four men, once labeled terrorists, were honored with Nobel Peace Prizes. Menachem Begin and Anwar Sadat shared one (1978) for brokering a peace treaty between Israel and Egypt.

AMERICA

Nelson Mandela (1994) was instrumental in leading South Africa to reconciliation. Yasser Arafat (1996), who remained in charge of the terrorist Palestine Liberation Organization (PLO), signed the Oslo Peace Accords (1993). They were all righteous acts, but they were off the hook for their past participation in terrorist activities.

Make of that what you will.

> *"Lots of countries, like Israel, live with terrorism every day, and it doesn't impact their integrity. The big threat to America is the way we react to terrorism by throwing away what everybody values about our country – a commitment to human rights. America is a great nation because we are a good nation."*
>
> **—Robert Kennedy, Jr.—**
> American environmental lawyer, author

Domestic terrorism includes white nationalism, neo-Nazism, anti-Muslim, anti-immigration, anti-LGBT, antisemitism, so-called anti-government "Patriot" movements, and individuals who commit crimes and violence because of personal grievances.

STANDING STRONG

How many American Asian citizens, for example, have been attacked in public during the pandemic? What did the attackers believe these Asian Americans had to do with the COVID virus? Label these attacks for what they are—domestic terrorism hate crimes. Wild conspiracy theories and misinformation is what influence many who commit hate crimes.

"Asymmetrical warfare is a euphemism for terrorism, just like collateral damage is a euphemism for killing innocent civilians."

—*Alan Dershowitz*—
American lawyer in U.S. constitutional law & American criminal law

An excerpt from ***A Field Guide to White Supremacy***, a book by *Kathleen Belew & **Ramon A. Gutierrez reinforces what we know; We read headlines and often skip the details. "Hate, racial violence, exclusion, and racist laws receive breathless media coverage, but such attention focuses on specific events that gain our attention for twenty-four hours. The events are presented as an episodic one-off, unfortunate but uncanny exception perpetrated by lone wolves, extremists, or

AMERICA

individuals suffering from mental illness—and then the news cycle moves on. If we turn to scholars and historians for background and answers, we often find their knowledge siloed in distinct academic subfields, rarely connecting current events with legal histories, nativist insurgencies, or centuries of misogynist, anti-Black, anti-Latino, anti-Asian, and xenophobic violence. But recent hateful actions are deeply connected to the past—joined not only by common perpetrators, but by the vast complex of systems, histories, ideologies, and personal beliefs that comprise white supremacy in the United States."

*Kathleen Belew is an assistant professor of history at the University of Chicago.
** Ramón Arturo Gutiérrez is an American the college at the University of Chicago. **"A Field Guide to White Supremacy"** is available at **Amazon.com**

> "The problem of domestic terrorism has been metastasizing across the country for a long time now, and it's not going away anytime soon. At the FBI, we've been sounding the alarm on it for a number of years.

—Christopher Wray—
Director, United States Federal Bureau of Investigation

STANDING STRONG

On August 12, 2017, few will soon forget the hate crime committed when Neo-Nazi and white supremacist groups invaded the University of Virginia campus, chanting anti-Semitic slogans, "Jews will not replace us." Before it was over, violence broke out. Nearby, a neo-Nazi named James Alex Fields Jr. drove his car into a crowd of protestors, injuring four people and killing 32-year-old Heather Heyer.

Three days later, on August 15th, the then president of the United States told a crowd. "You had some very bad people in that group, but you also had people that were very fine people, on both sides. You had people in that group, there were people in that rally — and I looked the night before — if you look, people were protesting the taking down of the statue of Robert E. Lee very quietly. I'm sure in that group there were some bad ones. The following day it looked like they had some rough, bad people — neo-Nazis, white nationalists, whatever you want to call them. But you had a lot of people in that group that was there to innocently protest and very legally protest."

The President's words were insulting, given that the August 12th video of the event confirmed otherwise.

AMERICA

The FBI lists neo-Nazi groups as domestic terrorists.

> *"For the last 20 years, our biggest concern was international terrorism — ISIS, Al Qaeda... Now it's here, and it's us, and it's the citizens of the United States, some of whom are rebelling against everything we thought we believed in for the last 300 to 400 years."*
>
> **—Bill Bratton—**
> Former New York City police commissioner

The FBI continues to issue warnings that domestic terrorists and those who spread misinformation and lies will not disappear. Some of these groups use technology to post lies and coded messages on Internet sites to apply their ideology. More than a few of these sites saw a rise in popularity following January 6, 2021, attack on the Capital. Why —had they heard a dog whistle telling them it was okay now?

"If you're talking about the lethality of the threat, domestic terrorism—meaning violent white supremacists, Neo-Nazis, sovereign citizens, militia movements—have been the most lethal threat in these past ten years compared to Al Qaeda and ISIS-inspired threats."

—Nate Snyder—
Former Homeland Security Department counterterrorism official

A Call to Action. What can we do about domestic terrorism? The National Strategy for Countering Domestic Terrorism offers the following: "We cannot ignore this threat or wish it away. Preventing domestic terrorism and reducing the factors that fuel it demand a multifaceted response across the Federal Government and beyond. That includes working with our critical partners in state, local, tribal, and territorial governments and civil society, the private sector, academia, local communities, and our allies and foreign partners. We have to take both short–term steps to counter the genuine threats of today and longer-term measures to diminish the emerging threats of domestic terrorism tomorrow."

AMERICA

To learn more, Google: The National Strategy for Countering Domestic Terrorism 2021 report.

The **Consequences** of international and domestic terrorism affect us all. We can be aware of the dysfunctional personality traits of those who may be candidates to commit terrorist acts and report them to authorities. The following are warning signs.

> *Potential terrorists can suffer from psychiatric illnesses (PTSD, depression).
> *Nonspecific distress (symptoms without a specific diagnosis, such as demoralization, perceived stress, and negative affect).
> *Health problems and concerns (somatic complaints, sleep disruption, increased use of sick leave).
> *Chronic problems like social disruption, family conflict, financial and occupational stress).
> *Can cause widespread property damage and severe economic consequences.

On the 20th Anniversary of the 9/11

attacks, George W. Bush, the 43rd President of the United States, delivered the following message on terrorism:

"It would be a mistake to idealize the experience of those terrible events. All that many people could initially see was the brute randomness of death. All that many could feel was unearned suffering. All that many could hear was God's terrible silence. Many still struggle with a lonely pain that cuts deep within. As a nation, our adjustments have been profound. Many Americans struggled to understand why an enemy would hate us with such zeal. The security measures incorporated into our lives are both sources of comfort and reminders of our vulnerability. And we have seen growing evidence that the dangers to our country can come not only across borders but from the violence that gathers within. There is little cultural overlap between violent extremists abroad and violent extremists at home. But in their disdain for pluralism, in their disregard for human life, in their determination to defile national symbols, they are children of the same foul spirit. And it is our continuing duty to confront them. At a time when religious bigotry might have flowed freely, I saw Americans reject prejudice and embrace people of the Muslim faith. That is the nation I know. This is not mere nostalgia; it is the truest version of ourselves. It is what we have been -- and what we can be again."

The final word goes to our friend, Friedrich Nietzsche.

> *"Whoever fights monsters should see to it that in the process, he does not become a monster. And if you gaze long enough into an abyss, the abyss will gaze back into you."*

—*Friedrich Nietzsche*—
(1844 – 1900)
German philosopher, cultural critic, composer, poet, writer

America's Changing Demographics

"The bosom of America is open to receive not only the opulent and respected stranger, but the oppressed and persecuted of all Nations and Religions; whom we shall welcome to the participation of all our rights and privileges."

—*George Washington*—
(1732 – 1799)
1st President of the United States

That's who we are; that's who we need to remain if we hope to uphold our commitment to democracy. America's changing demographics are a *fait accompli,* and they always were from the beginning. If anyone doubts that a significant change is taking place, turn on the TV. Corporate TV commercials regularly present all races and all ethnicities. As corporate America goes, so goes America. It is the same with entertainment, which has become all-inclusive, representing all races and ethnicities.

Progress.

The latest statistics from ***Pew Research Project** indicate that "The nation will become 'Minority White' as soon as 2045. During that year, whites will comprise 49.7 percent of the population in contrast to 24.6 percent for Hispanics,13,1 percent for black, 7.9 percent for Asians, and 3.8 percent for multiracial populations."

To read the complete Pew Research report, Google: **Youthful minorities are the engine of the future.**

To some, the above statistics are a bridge too far, and they will do whatever is necessary to stop the trend or slow it down, whether it be a change in immigration laws, state voting laws, or whatever else they can conjure up to skirt existing laws.

Unless one is a descendant of Native Americans, none of us have the right to claim this land as ours and ours alone. Our immigrant ancestors made it possible for all of us to be here. Period, full stop.

Flash forward to 2022, when anti-immigrant voices were rising. Senator Romney dared to speak words of inclusion.

"We are a nation of immigrants. We are the children and grandchildren and great-grandchildren of the ones who wanted a better life, the driven ones, the ones who woke up at night hearing that voice telling them that life in a place called America could be better."

—*Mitt Romney*—
United States Senator from Utah

Let's begin by debunking the most common arguments posed by those who target specific groups of immigrants. In a Cato Institute article titled "***The Most Common Arguments Against Immigration and Why They're Wrong***," *Alex Nowrasteh writes, "Arguments against immigration come across my desk every day, but I rarely encounter a unique one. In 2016, I wrote a blog responding to the most common arguments linked to additional research. These are the main arguments against immigration."

"Immigrants will take American jobs, lower our wages, and especially hurt the poor."

AMERICA

"Immigrants abuse the welfare state."

"Immigrants increase the budget deficit and government debt."

"Immigrants increase economic inequality."

"Today's immigrants don't assimilate like immigrants from previous waves did."

"Immigrants are a major source of crime."

"Immigrants pose a unique risk today because of terrorism."

"It's easy to immigrate to America, and we're the most open country in the world."

"Amnesty or a failure to enforce our immigration laws will destroy the Rule of Law in the United States."

[A threat to] **"National sovereignty."**

"Immigrants bring with them their bad cultures, ideas, or other factors that will undermine and destroy our economic and political institutions.

"The brain drain of smart immigrants to the United States impoverished other countries."

STANDING STRONG

"Immigrants will increase crowding, harm the environment, and [insert misanthropic statement here]."

Mr. Nowrasteh further explains: "There are other arguments that are regularly used in opposition to immigration. Many revolve around issues of "fairness"—a word with a fuzzy meaning that differs dramatically among people and cultures. Arguments about fairness depend entirely upon feelings and, usually, a misunderstanding of the facts that is usually corrected by reference to my 8th point above. These are the main arguments against immigration that I encounter and my quick responses."

Alexander Nowrasteh is an American analyst of immigration policy currently working at the Center for Global Liberty and Prosperity of the Cato Institute in Washington, D.C.

For the answers to the questions posed, Google: ***The 14 Most Common Arguments against Immigration and Why They're Wrong.***

"No matter who you are or what you look like, how you started off, or how and who you love, America is a place where you can write your own destiny."

—*President Barack Obama*—

44th President of the United States

AMERICA

Everyone agrees that we need solid immigration laws for anyone who wishes to come to America. There is some positive news on the immigration front with that in mind. A poll confirms that two-thirds of Americans, on the left and the right, agree that immigration is essential to who America was and remains. Those who continue to view the influx of some "problematic nationalities" are the same people who spread racism. If it looks like a duck, walks like a duck, it's a duck.

> *"We have become not a melting pot but a beautiful mosaic. Different people, different beliefs, different yearnings, different hopes, different dreams."*
>
> **—President Jimmy Carter—**
> 39th President of the United States

There isn't much more to add to this conversation. We're all aware of what's going on with white supremacists, neo-Nazis, and hate groups. They take full advantage of the 1st Amendment, speaking and acting openly with attacks against anyone who doesn't look like them, think like them, or act like them. Thankfully, they represent a minority voice with no actual standing in today's society—that is, if we stand firm against them.

A call to action. What can we do to ensure assimilation with a changing and diverse America? Support our original values. America became a free and democratic country by opening its borders to new faces, new voices, and new talent.

The **Consequences** of denying immigration.

>*Research confirms immigration leads to more innovation, a better-educated workforce, greater occupational specialization, better matching skills with jobs, and higher overall economic productivity. Immigration also has a net positive effect on combined federal, state, and local budgets.
>*Immigrants contribute to the U.S. economy and economic output by increasing the size of the labor force and increasing productivity.
>*Population growth through immigration adds to additional

increases in per-capita income in models where specific sectors of the economy become more efficient at higher production levels.

*More significant increases in immigration—enabling more than 2 million immigrants each year to come to the U.S.—would lead to a $2,500 increase in GDP per capita by 2050.

The final word goes to the 40th President of the United States.

"I received a letter just before I left office from a man. I don't know why he chose to write it, but I'm glad he did. He wrote that you can go to live in France, but you can't become a Frenchman. You can go to live in Germany or Italy, but you can't become a German or Italian. He went through Turkey, Greece, Japan, and other countries. But he said anyone, from any corner of the world, can come to live in the United States and become an American."

—President Ronald Reagan—

STANDING STRONG

(1911–2004)
40th President of the United States

We transition to events that we as individuals do have some level of control over whether we choose to exercise it or not.

Between 2015 and 2021, America experienced a series of jarring events that have brought us to this troubling moment in time, a moment of fear followed by reflection and definitions that hopefully will assist us in going forward. How we might have dealt with these events differently remains the question we all have to answer.

Each day we make dozens of decisions, big and small, that affect how we get through our day and the days and weeks ahead. No matter how insignificant, each decision brings a positive or negative consequence. As we will explore, those are the times that require us to exercise personal responsibility when our choices might affect others negatively.

Read on with an open mind.

AMERICA

"What you leave behind is not what is engraved in stone monuments, but what is woven into the lives of others."

—*Pericles*—

(Born: Athens, Greece – Died 429BC)
Greek statesman and general prominent & influential in Athenian politics -acclaimed by Thucydides, a contemporary historian, as "the first citizen of Athens"

Anger & The Loss of Civility

"If the great American people will only keep their temper on both sides of the line, our troubles will come to an end."

—Abraham Lincoln—
(1809 -1865)
16th President of the United States

What went wrong, and what went right.

Imagine that we lived in a world where everyone was selfish (perish the thought) with no regard for anyone's personal feelings, where rudeness and incivility were not only encouraged but acceptable behavior.

Okay, that was a bit of a stretch, my bad. But since the pandemic and a few other painful events along the way, anger and incivility have been on display more than usual. Why?

AMERICA

"What is tolerance? It is the consequence of humanity. We are all formed of frailty and error; let us pardon reciprocally each other's folly –that is the first flaw of nature."

—Voltaire—
(1694 -1778)
Writer, historian & philosopher

The expression of anger, incivility, and hubris gets us nowhere since those on the receiving end of our ire get angry at us. We end up yelling past one another, spitting out quick rebuttals to barely heard comments that guarantee neither party gets their point across.

"Manners is what holds a society together."

—Jane Austen—
(1775 – 1817)
English novelist best known for her six major novels

Psychologists believe we're influenced from early childhood by the steady stream of violence, gore, and terror in our films, TV programs, and computer games. Studies link people who feast on violent entertainment with increased aggression and anger. Psychologists say that these folks also have trouble expressing empathy for the suffering of others and are less willing to assist those in need help.

> *"Anger, like a fire, is a primal force. When left unchecked, it can be destructive, yet when managed and used wisely, it can be a beneficial and powerful instrument that leads to enlightenment."*
>
> ***—Moshe Ratson—***
> Executive Coach, Psychotherapist, Anger Management & Marriage Therapist in New York City

The uptick in anger can be traced to when our political scene grew even more polarized than it had been, quickly followed by a pandemic that hit like a category five hurricane. Then came the George Floyd murder, followed by the Black Lives Matter Movement, the 2020 election, the attack on the capital, anger against those who refused to get vaccinated, protests against the shutdowns and COVID mandates, and the backup in the supply chain leading to severe inflation, and of course, the looming effects of climate change. It felt like Armageddon lurked just inside the earth's atmosphere, waiting to rain down on us.

> *"When angry, count to ten before you speak. If very angry, count to one hundred."*
>
> **—*Thomas Jefferson*—**
> (1743 – 1826)
> 3rd President of the United States

We were frustrated with everything happening and allowed our anger to spill over to others. In Nancy Gibbs's article in the Washington Post, she explains what we were feeling and how we vented in public. "Last year (2021) just made us meaner — to shop clerks and flight attendants, teachers and nurses, election officials and our fellow citizens — really anyone forced to leave their foxholes," she wrote. "We fought over everything, including why we fight so much. We thought we were liberated from the pandemic, only to be tackled and dragged back into its cages; we exited Afghanistan; we watched lawmakers fall and flounder as if their shoelaces were tied together. Every day was a feast for the outrage industry, for candidates and cable networks and platform companies that we learned for years gave five times the algorithmic weight to posts that set us off. We've apparently developed a taste for bile."

<u>Nancy Reid Gibbs is an American essayist, speaker, and presidential historian. To read the article Google:</u> **<u>2021 made us meaner. Can 2022 be a year of second chances?</u>**

"Anybody can become angry, that is easy, but to be angry with the right person and to the right degree and at the right time and for the right purpose, and in the right way, that is not within everybody's power and is not easy."

—*Aristotle*—
(384 BC – 322 BC)
Greek philosopher and polymath during
The Classical period in Ancient Greece

Like all our emotions, anger triggers the body's fight or flight response that can all too often turn into violence. An example is the violent outbreaks on planes. Since Jan. 1, 2022, the FAA has recorded 394 reported incidents on flights nationwide; 255 of those were related to face mask mandates. Our adrenal glands are on speed, flooding us with stress hormones, and if it leads to physical aggression, we're ready for it. But over a mask that protects the wearer and those, they come in contact with? Not acceptable. Look at the rise in road rage incidents that turned violent.

> *"What is more cruel than anger? What is more affectionate to others than man? Yet what is more savage against them than anger? Mankind is born for mutual assistance, anger for mutual ruin.*
>
> ***—Seneca—***
> (Date born unknown – died 65AD)
> Lucius Annaeus Seneca the Younger,
> Roman Stoic philosopher, statesman, dramatist

*Hannah Devlin, a London-based science correspondent, weighs in on the question of rising anger levels in her article in **TheGuardian.com.** "Science is beginning to provide new explanations about the ways that personality, age, gender, and life experiences shape the way we feel this emotion. Whether we end up swearing or scowling, or even punching someone depends on a second brain area, the prefrontal cortex, that is responsible for decision-making and reasoning. This puts our anger in context, reminds us to behave in socially acceptable ways, and for most of us, most of the time keeps our primal instincts in check."

*<u>Hannah Devlin is the Guardian's science correspondent, a Ph.D. in biomedical imaging from the University of Oxford, and presents the Science Weekly podcast. To read the article, Google: **Science of Anger: How gender, age, and personality shape this emotion.**</u>

> *"I really believe that all of us have a lot of darkness in our souls. Anger, rage, fear, sadness. I don't think that's only reserved for people who had a horrible upbringing. I think it really exists and is part of the human condition. I think in the course of your life, you figure out ways to deal with that."*
>
> **—*Kevin Bacon*—**
> American Actor Extraordinaire

AMERICA

Some do, Kevin, and some don't. And yet, most people are aware that incivility only leads to more of the same. The way to handle the problem is to listen to our prefrontal cortex and think before speaking. Consider a bit of humor as an alternative way to get our point across—assuming we have a valid one—and before you know it, mission accomplished without trading insults.

> *"Darkness cannot drive out darkness; only light can do that. Hate cannot drive out hate; only love can do that. Hate multiplies hate, violence multiplies violence, and toughness multiplies toughness in a descending spiral of destruction. The Chain reaction of evil – hate begetting hate, wars producing more wars—must be broken, or we shall be plunged into the dark abyss of annihilation."*

—*Martin Luther King, Jr.*—
(1929 – 1968)
Baptist Minister and Activist in the civil rights movement

STANDING STRONG

It would be fair to blame our anger on the pain and suffering that came our way in recent years. But, wait, not so fast. Jennifer Rubin, a columnist for The New York Times, writes that it began earlier. "The problem started long before... Back in 2013, studies were warning that civility in America continued to disintegrate and rude behavior was becoming the new normal. The report 'Civility in America 2019' found that 93 percent of Americans identified incivility as a problem; 68 percent considered it a 'major' one, and 74 percent thought it was getting worse."

Jennifer Rubin is an American political commentator who writes opinion columns for The Washington Post. To read the article, Google: **Americans' behavior gets worse. No wonder our politics are lousy.**

"Civility, politeness, it's like cement in a society: binds it together. And when we lose it, then I think we all feel lesser and slightly dirty because of it."

—*Jeremy Irons*—
Academy Award-winning English actor and activist

Why rude behavior has been increasing since 2013 is anyone's guess. It only adds fuel to an already out-of-control flame. And as we all know; apologies are hard to come by. Have you ever uncounted a stranger who did or said something rude that you boldly pointed out only to get their middle finger tossed at you instead of an apology? If everyday kindness and civility were hard to come before, apologies are... *forgetaboutit*!

> *"Speak when you are angry, and you will make the best speech you will ever regret."*
>
> **—*Ambrose Bierce*—**
> (1842 – 1941)
> American short-story writer, journalist, poet, and a Civil War veteran

A Call to Action. What are the best ways of controlling our anger? Think before we speak. It will save us from embarrassment and the hurt feelings of others. It's no more complicated than that. If in doubt, re-read this chapter, and let's try to get a grip on our anger.

The **Consequences** of expressing anger and

<u>incivility.</u>

>*It leads to emotional tension and mental strain on both the abuser and receiver.
>*High levels of stress and the onset of depression can result if we let our anger get the best of us.
>*Anxiety and feelings of overwhelming dread when we are uncivil.
>*Radical mood swings lead to more anger.
>*Uncontrolled anger often leads to some form of violence.
>*It often leads to online cyberbullying.
>*Anger directed toward a spouse is the worst. Since you both live under the same roof, expressed anger lingers and festers and leads to more anger.

The final word goes to NBC newsman Tom Brokaw.

AMERICA

"My hope is that we would begin to have a dialogue in this country about the importance of civility. We can have strong differences, but it does seem to me that most of the country believes it's gone to critical mass in what I would call the professional class across the political spectrum left and right."

—*Tom Brokaw*—
American network television journalist and author

Whatever Happened to Common Sense?

"Common sense is something that everyone needs, few have, and none think they lack."

—Benjamin Franklin—
(1706 – 1790)
American writer, scientist, inventor, statesman, diplomat, printer, publisher, and political philosopher

What went wrong, and what went right.

Here we go again with yet another disturbing human paradox. Medical science blames the use or non-use of common sense on our prefrontal cortex again, which is also responsible for making us aware of the consequences if we don't. So, no snap or knee-jerk decisions are allowed. Solution: stop, think, then speak.

AMERICA

"I read, I study, I examine, I listen, I think, and out of all that I try to form an idea into which I put as much common sense as I can."

—Marquis de Lafayette—
(1757 – 1834)
French aristocrat and military officer who fought in the American Revolutionary War commanding American troop

Our ability to exercise common sense is supposed to improve as we age. Yeah, well, for some, it does; for others, not so much. Engaging this wonder tool called common sense before setting loose our voice box keeps us from making errors we might come to regret. Like lawyer, writer, and orator Robert Green Ingersoll (1833 – 1899) wisely said, "It is a thousand times better to have common sense without education than education without common sense."

Translations: That expensive college degree doesn't guarantee that one's common sense has improved if one didn't have it, to begin with. We all know a few—well, maybe more than a few—who have impressive college pedigrees but who time and again fail the common-sense test. Trying to get through to them on the most straightforward issues is often impossible. Go ahead, name a few in Congress that come to mind.

Let's take this one step further with *Stef Daniel, who minces no words in her article on the online blog ***Professorshouse.com***. "What is it about society today that makes thinking and acting like a complete idiot an okay thing to do? Where have our morals gone? Why does no one believe in karma anymore? Why is doing the right thing so difficult for so many? When will we, as a society, learn that the most valuable asset we have to offer this world and those around us is the ability of the human brain to use common sense? Seriously, what happened to common freaking sense?"

*Stef Daniel is the experienced mother of 4 daughters who has taught her nearly everything she needs to know about raising kids and staying sane. To read the entire Google: **What Happened to Common Sense – Are People Really that Clueless?**

> *"Common sense is like deodorant.*
> *The people who need it most*
> *never use it."*
>
> **—Bill Murry—**
> Actor, comedian, and writer

AMERICA

Albert Einstein, who knew a lot of really cool stuff, had his own theory on the subject when he said, "Common sense is the collection of prejudices acquired by the age of eighteen."

With the current generation, the age has been lowered to fifteen.

We end this chapter with a prime example of how not using common sense got one January 6th Capital insurrectionist in a heap of trouble.

Thirty-six-year-old Adam Johnson pleaded guilty to storming the U.S. Capital and taking House Speaker Nancy Pelosi's lectern and parading it around like it was the horse's head from the scene in "The Godfather." Here, for our enjoyment, is the exchange between Mr. Johnson and U. S. District Court Judge Reggie Walton.

<u>JUDGE WALTON:</u> "It's very concerning to me that you were weak-minded enough that you would follow a lie and do what you did. So why shouldn't I lock you up, sir? Why should I think you won't do this again?"

<u>MR. JOHNSON:</u> "I've spent a lot of time listening to a lot of information, reading a lot of things, and I think maybe your assessment is accurate that I got caught up in a moment.

Your honor, I understand that my actions are regrettable. I'm here pleading guilty because I am guilty."

Mr. Johnson appears to have been a dollar short and a day late when exercising his innate common-sense abilities before following an angry, violent, lied-to crowd that landed him in trouble with the law.

We humans are flawed, limited, and finite; this we know. But our shortcomings when it comes to anger and civility are one of our controllable emotions. That separates us from those chimpanzees who insisted to primatologist and anthropologist Jane Goodall one day that they, not humans, were the masters of the Earth.

Make of that what you will.

"The three great essentials to achieve anything worthwhile are, first, hard work; second, stick-to-itiveness; third, common sense."

—*Thomas A Edison*—
(1847 – 1931)
Credited with many inventions, including the incandescent light bulb & the phonograph. He held over 1,000 patents for his designs.

Call to Action. What can we do to ensure we exercise common sense when making critical decisions? We often look for things that are not there when the answer is simple. Stop, think, be sure we know what we are talking about, then act. Only then can we be sure we are exercising ordinary sound judgment. We all have it, but many fail to use it.

The **Consequences** of not exercising common sense.

>*Quick opinions and decisions often backfire.
>*It is a danger to others who may follow our advice.
>*Being labeled as someone who is not to be engaged in serious discussions.
>*Being viewed as someone who fails to check facts and stubbornly refuses to accept them when presented.
>*No one wants to be proven wrong. To avoid that is to use common sense and check facts first.

The final word goes to philosopher Voltaire.

STANDING STRONG

"What is tolerance? It is the consequence of humanity. We are all formed of frailty and error; let us pardon reciprocally each other's folly – that is the first law of nature."

—*Voltaire*—
(1694 -1778)
Writer, historian, and philosopher

AMERICA

Racism in America

"As long as people can be judged by the color of their skin, the problem is not solved.

—Oprah Winfrey—
Talk show host, TV producer, actress, Author and philanthropist

What went right, and what went wrong.

Racism is self-defeating. It confirms the un-enlightenment (excellent way to put it) of those who believe they are better than others. It is problematic for some to reject beliefs they may have learned at a young age. But it's never too late to see life through a different lens that shines a light on the truth, facts, and understanding. To commit a hate crime based on an individual's disability, gender, nationality, race, ethnicity, religion, or sexual orientation is unacceptable and hypocritical because everyone falls into at least one category.

STANDING STRONG

"The function of racism... is a distraction. It keeps you from doing your work. It keeps you explaining, over and over again, your reason for being. Somebody says you have no language, and so you spend 20 years proving that you do. None of that is necessary. There will always be one more thing."

—Toni Morrison—
(1931 – 2019)
Critically acclaimed American novelist

Senator Mitt Romney's verbal slap at his fellow Republican senators is as good a place to continue this discussion.

During an interview with CNN's Dana Bash on the **State of the Union** program, Senator Romney of Utah blasted his fellow party members who attended a White Nationalist event. "Look," Senator Romney said, "there is no place in either political party for this White nationalism or racism. It's simply wrong; it's evil as well. I'm reminded of that old line from the 'Butch Cassidy and the Sundance Kid' movie where - where one character says, 'Morons, I've got morons on my team.' And I have to think anybody that would sit down with White nationalists and speak at their conference was certainly missing a few IQ points."

Romney's message applies to anyone who would knowingly and purposely usher a racist comment. The same goes for members of Congress who attend and support a white nationalist movement. They're free to participate if they like, but it raises a serious question of who they are and are these the people we want in high-level elected positions.

> *"Prejudice is a burden that confuses the past, threatens the future, and renders the present inaccessible."*
>
> ***—Maya Angelou—***
> (1928 – 2014)
> American poet, memoirist, and civil rights activist

To the chagrin of many, science has confirmed we are all biologically the same despite some who continue to victimize others who, in their mind, are members of inferior races. There are no inferior races, only the human race. No one individual or group has evidence to the contrary. We may look different and speak differently, but that is evolution's doing.

STANDING STRONG

An article in ***world-Mysteries.com*** sets the record straight. "The human race is defined as a group of people with certain common inherited features that distinguish them from other groups of people. All men of whatever race are currently classified by the anthropologist or biologist as belonging to the one species, Homo sapiens. This is another way of saying that the differences between human races are not great, even though they may appear so, i.e., black vs. white skin. All races of humanity in the world can interbreed because they have so much in common. All races share 99.99+% of the same genetic materials which means that division of race is largely subjective and that the original 3-5 races were also probably just subjective descriptions as well... The notion that humankind can be divided along white, black, and yellow lines reveal the social rather than the scientific origin of race... Referents of terms like Black, White, Asian, and Latino are social groups, not genetically distinct branches of humankind... By 1871, some leading intellectuals had recognized that even using the word 'race' was virtually a confession of ignorance or evil intent... Unfortunately, few in this society seem prepared to fully relinquish their subscription to notions of biological race."

As always, some will agree, others not so

much. Their loss.

To read the article, Google: **How many major races are there in the world?**

> *"Anyone who continues to believe in race as a physical attribute of individuals, despite the now commonplace disclaimers of biologists and geneticists might as well also, believe in the Santa Clause, the Easter Bunny, and the tooth fairy is real, and that the earth stands still while the sun moves."*
>
> **—Barbara Jeanne Fields—**
> Professor of American history at Columbia University

And yet, given the above scientific facts, racism persists. Why? Why do so many reject the truth that we are all the same despite one's color or ethnicity? Racism marks the bias of individuals who cannot move past their prejudices.

An excerpt from an article from the ***Goldwater Institute** takes it one step further with an explanation of the currently popular subject—at least in some quarters—

of critical race theory.

"Critical Race Theory is a perspective on modern life—a worldview—that believes all the events and ideas around us in politics, education, entertainment, the media, the workplace, and beyond must be explained in terms of racial identities.... Critical Race Theorists reject the idea that people should be judged based on their character, insisting they be judged instead only on their identities, rejecting the Civil Rights-era notion of colorblindness. They developed the notion of "intersectionality," where you can identify with more than one group to claim additional social benefits. Further, theorists say that the U.S. Constitution and system of laws cannot be neutral, giving rise to the idea of 'systemic racism'... All of these concepts create a culture of fear, where Americans are told to focus on their differences and to reward victimization. Even worse, Critical Race Theory sets up people for failure by telling certain individuals that America was not created for them—that the American Dream was never theirs—when, in fact, life, liberty, and the pursuit of happiness are promised to *all* Americans, regardless of gender, color, or social circumstance."

Let's assume that most of us are open-minded about new immigration and are willing to accept America's changing demographics and assimilate. In that case, Google: * ***The New Social Justice Makes Everyone Guilty: A Primer on Critical Race Theory***. This article is a must-read.

> *"I am for the immediate, unconditional, and universal enfranchisement of the black man in every state in the union. Without this, his liberty is a mockery; Without this, you might as well almost retain the old name of slavery for his condition."*

—Frederick Douglas—
(1818 – 1895)
Former enslave, abolitionist, author & activist

The problem can be traced to the founding fathers. They struck a compromise when drafting the final version of the Constitution. Some framers of the Constitution were against slavery. Others were enslavers who viewed their laborers as personal and financial assets. Despite this dichotomy, those against slavery gave into slaveholding states to ensure the Constitution would get ratified. Over time, seventeen hundred members of the United States Congress owned enslaved people. America was a racially divided nation from the beginning of our democracy.

> *"There is no vaccine for racism. We've got to do the work for George Floyd, Breonna Taylor, and the lives of too many others to name. We've got to do the work to fulfill that promise of equal justice under the law. Because none of us are free until all of us are free."*
>
> ***—Kamala Harris—***
> Vice President of the United States

In 2021, Attorney General, Merrick Garland, stated, "Hate crimes instill fear across entire communities." Garland said he was rededicating the Justice Departments' efforts in combatting hate and bias-related incidents and directed the FBI to increase efforts to educate and encourage the public to report hate and racial crimes to law enforcement.

The First Amendment of the Constitution covers hate speech. It states that racism *"maybe is"* punishable if the act provokes an attack or is otherwise threatening beyond insulting a person or group based on national origin, ethnicity, color, religion, gender, gender identity, sexual orientation, or disability. Maybe?

AMERICA

Hate crimes in our country have reached the highest level in the past twelve years. That's not progress; it is shameful backwardness. We can help curb this trend by not looking the other way. When we see something and fail to report it, it just continues.

> *"There are huge divorces and divides and chasms in black America between the have-gots and the have-nots, between the monied and the poor, between the educated and the non-educated. And there are huge and growing chasms daily. And I want to say that it's not simply about generation. It's about genre."*

—*Neil deGrasse Tyson*—
American Astrophysicist

A Call to Action. What can we do to fight continued racism? Support the changing demographics of America that have constantly changed from the country's inception. Effective change to end racism begins with education, equal opportunities, and the will to speak up against discrimination when we see it. A significant step would be to stop using certain words like black, brown, yellow, Asian, and Latinos, or the first black or the first Hispanic to achieve whatever. It's degrading. We are all the "Human Race," the one actual race.

The **Consequences** of racism and the price we pay.

*Racism attributes to the increase in hate crimes, hate groups, and violence.
*Racism attempts to rewrite American history falsely.
*Racism prevents people from reaching their economic potential.
*Racism carries high adverse economic costs to everyone. A less racist society is an economically stronger one. Citigroup, for example, placed a price tag on how much the economy has lost as a result of discrimination against African Americans: $16 trillion. Not exactly loose change.
*Institutionalized racism has been defined as "the structures, policies, practices, and norms resulting in differential access to society's goods, services, and opportunities by race. That helps no one.

AMERICA

The final word goes to former First Lady Michelle Obama.

> *"I can't make people not afraid of black people. I don't know what's going on. I can't explain what's happening in your head. But maybe if I show up every day as a human, a good human, doing wonderful things, loving my family, loving your kids, taking care of things that I care about— maybe, just maybe, that work will pick away at the scabs of your discrimination. Maybe that slowly will unravel it. That's all we have because we can't do it for them because they're broken. Their brokenness in how they see us is a reflection of this brokenness. And you can't fix that. All you can do is the work.*

—*Michelle Obama*—
Former First Lady of the United States

Guns In America

In addition to needed gun control reforms, America urgently needs a stronger protest movement dedicated to reducing the glorification of violence in our culture - in music, film, television, video games, and even the Internet.

—Bernice King—
American lawyer, minister & youngest child of civil rights leaders Martin Luther King Jr. and Coretta Scott King

What went wrong, and what went right.

On April 21st, 2022, The Washington Post ran an article on recent shootings that left numerous people dead or injured. Officials said the gunfire appeared to be tied to disputes among people or groups in public or crowded areas. This violence underscores how shootings are up significantly compared with before the pandemic. The ongoing toll has public officials and others fearful heading into the summer months. And yet, knowing full well that we have a gun problem in America, some states controlled by conservative legislatures are passing laws allowing anyone of age to get a weapon without a permit. How does this make sense when we need common-sense gun laws to protect the public? Everyone should read this article and be aware.

To read the article by Mark Berman, Joanna Slater, Griff Witte, and Andrew Ba Tran, Google: ***As shootings mount, anger grows that it's 'happening over and over.***

There is some good news coming out of the White House. President Biden has reiterated his call for Congress to pass commonsense gun violence prevention legislation, which fully aligns with the Second Amendment. If passed, the legislation would require background checks for all gun sales, a ban on assault weapons and high-capacity magazines, the repeal of gun manufacturers' protection from liability, and the banning of ghost guns. The majority of Americans support Biden's proposal. It is now up to Congress to take action. Let's see how far this proposal gets since Congress remains reluctant to do what it should have done years ago.

STANDING STRONG

"The Constitution of most of our states... and of the United States... assert that all power is inherently in the people; that they may exercise it by themselves; that it is their right and duty to be at all times armed."
—Thomas Jefferson—
(1743 – 1826)
Third President of the United States

Fair enough, Mr. Jefferson. However, since you've been gone, things have gotten a bit out of hand regarding gun violence and how to deal with it effectively. There are over 400 million privately owned firearms in the United States, with somewhere between one-third and one-half of American households owning at least one. So, Mr. Jefferson, we have our hands full until we get around to passing common-sense gun laws.

"There are no free and democratic and wealthy countries in the world that have the U.S. rate of gun violence. We have to worry about loners and alienated people. We have to do better on mental health."
—David Brooks—
A political and cultural commentator for
The New York Times

AMERICA

In an article in ***Everytownresearch.org,*** the Centers for Disease Control and Prevention announced the first US death from COVID-19 on March 1, 2020. One year later, there were over 28.7 million cases in the United States and 515,700 deaths. Over this same period, the gun violence epidemic surged. Many Americans who purchased guns felt they had to protect themselves, partially in response to gun lobby propaganda that social unrest was inevitable and that the government would not protect them. Unfortunately, some people responded to these messages. Throughout 2020, federally licensed gun dealers requested nearly 40 million background checks—40 percent more than during 2019.

*To read the article, Google: **Gun Violence and COVID-19 in 2020.***

With the above information readily available, we have to repeat the question: Why have some 20 states passed laws or are considering laws allowing people to walk around with a gun without a permit? Vehicle drivers have to have a license, and many states require a permit to hunt and fish. Why would we loosen gun laws to make it easier for humans to kill other humans? It also places police officers at significant risk of not knowing who may be carrying a weapon.

Welcome to America, the wild, wild West, when it comes to common-sense gun laws. It makes no sense. When is enough... *enough*?

> *"The number of Americans killed since 9-11 by terrorism is less than 100. If you look at the number that has been killed by gun violence, it's in the tens of thousands."*
>
> **—*Barack Obama*—**
> 44th President of the United States

Opponents of common-sense gun regulation argue, as they always have, that the proposed new laws would infringe on the 2nd Amendment. They make the argument that armed citizens stop mass murders. That is false. Statistics issued by the FBI prove otherwise. The answer is always the same with these contentious issues; *Follow the money.* You don't need to be a brainiac to know that current laws protect the NRA, the gun manufacturers, and the elected officials who protect both. *Follow the money.*

AMERICA

"Only with gun violence do we respond to repeated tragedies by saying that mourning is acceptable but discussing how to prevent more tragedies is not. But that's unacceptable. As others have observed, talking about how to stop a mass shooting in the aftermath of a string of mass shootings isn't 'too soon.' It's much too late."

—*Ezra Klein*—
Journalist, political analyst, New York Times columnist - host of The Ezra Klein Show podcast & co-founder of Vox

Most gun rights activists argue that "a good guy with a gun" can save people from gun violence. Studies have confirmed again and again that this is false. The FBI reports that a privately owned weapon rarely prevents violence. It is more likely that a gun in the home will be used for suicide or homicide than self-defense. That is a fact that has been confirmed time and again.

Make of that what you will.

On November 23, 2021, U.S. Senator Chris Murphy delivered these remarks on the

Senate floor following the tragic shooting at Oxford High School in Michigan, leaving three students dead and eight others injured.

"Do not lecture us about the sanctity, the importance of life when one hundred people every single day are losing their lives to guns when kids go to school fearful that they won't return home because a classmate will turn a gun on them when it is in our control whether this happens. Do you care about life? Then get these dangerous military-style weapons off the streets, out of our schools. Do you care about life? Make sure that criminals don't get guns by making sure that everybody goes through a background check in this country... This only happens in the United States of America. There's no other nation in the high-income world in which kids worry about being shot when they go to school. It happens here in America because we choose to let it happen. We're not unlucky. This is purposeful. This is a choice made by the United States Senate to sit on our hands and do nothing while kids die. It doesn't even involve any political risk. The changes we're talking about to make our schools safe places they're supported by the vast majority of Americans, Republicans and Democrats... I think about [gun violence] first and foremost as a parent of a 7th grader and a 4th grader who are part of a generation that accepts as part of their childhood the risk of not leaving school at the end of the day because of a violent attack. That's the reality of being a kid in school today. I'm angry about it as an American, but I'm angry about it as a parent that my children have to go through active shooter drills because this has become a regular facet of being a child in America, exposure to gun violence. I'm beyond my tipping point. But I needed to come to the floor today because having sat in that chair listening to my colleagues tell me about how much they care about human life, well, you have an opportunity to do something about it. You have an opportunity to save lives right now. Kids that are walking into schools tomorrow need you, need you to step up and pass laws that are going to make sure that only responsible people own guns."

Common sense gun laws protect everyone, including responsible gun owners. The only way to protect the 2nd Amendment is to pass laws protecting gun owners and the public from the insane amount of gun violence America experiences every day.

STANDING STRONG

"Our Second Amendment is freedom's most valuable, most cherished, most irreplaceable idea. History proves it. When you ignore the right of good people to own firearms to protect their freedom, you become the enablers of future tyrants whose regimes will destroy millions and millions of defenseless lives."

—*Wayne LaPierre*—
Executive vice president and CEO,
National Rifle Association

Mr. LaPierre's remarks to justify the number of guns in circulation, plus the ones we don't know about, are shamefully self-serving and nothing more than a PR and scare tactic.

"I'll give you my gun when you pry it from my cold, dead hands."

—*Charlton Heston, Actor*—
(1923 – 2008)
Spoken like a true movie icon at the
129th NRA Convention

AMERICA

Great way to kick off an NRA convention and rile up members in attendance with a real he-man movie star holding a rifle over his head, challenging anyone to pry it from his hands.

As for the *NRA's* role in all this, *Rukmani Bhatia wrote for **The Center for American Progress**: "Due to the insidious nature of this messaging approach, the NRA has successfully embedded its false narrative throughout much of the country. By deploying a carefully crafted campaign of misinformation, deception, and confusion, the NRA has both undermined legitimate arguments for common-sense gun law reform and made it substantially more difficult for its emotive, provocative propaganda to be countered with fact and reason... The propaganda machine of the NRA is similar to that of authoritarian and undemocratic political regimes around the world that deploy disinformation campaigns to secure control over public discourse in their nations, enabling autocrats to maintain a vice grip over information and ensure their power is unchecked and unquestioned."

Rukmani Bhatia is the senior policy analyst for Gun Violence Prevention at the Center for American Progress. To read the article, Google: **Guns, lies, and Fear – Exposing the NRA's Messaging Playbook.

STANDING STRONG

"Making improvements to our background check system and cracking down on illegal gun trafficking is common-sense ways to prevent violence without punishing the law-abiding gun owners. We owe it to the American people to take real action to reduce gun violence in our communities."

—Martin Heinrich—
American politician serving as the senior United States senator from New Mexico

According to a Pew Research Center survey, Americans who favor stricter gun laws are rising. 60% of Americans agree that gun laws should be more rigid. Then why aren't they? We need only to look to Congress, which continually turns a deaf ear despite what the majority of the public wants. Perhaps we have the wrong people in Congress who blatantly disregard the wants and needs of those who elected them in exchange for whatever benefits, including financial, Congressional members may receive by going against public will. Common sense tells us there is a middle ground where the 2nd Amendment is protected, and people are protected from the ever-growing gun incident in the U.S. America, with its archaic gun laws, does indeed resemble the wild, wild West.

> *"I'm a teacher, and every time I hear a loud noise in the hall, I wonder if my time is up. My wife is also a teacher. I worry about her every day. Why is this our reality? Why do my students have to live this way?"*
>
> —*@TheReelRandom*—

In her book, **Kurt Vonnegut, Writing with Style,** *Susanne McConnell's quoted a passage from Vonnegut's novel **Deadeye Dick** that fits this urgent issue like a glove even though it is fiction.

"At the age of 11, this kid was playing with one of his father's guns, which he wasn't supposed to do, put a cartridge into a 30-06 rifle and fired out a goddamn attic window and killed a housewife, you know, eighteen blocks away, just drilled her right between the eyes. And this has colored his whole life and made his reputation. And, of course, this weapon should not have existed. He was brought into (a) planet where this terrible unstable device existed, and all he had to do was sneeze near it. I mean, it wanted to be fired; it was built to be fired. It had no other purpose than to be fired, and the existence of such an unstable device within the reach of any sort of human being is intolerable."

*<u>Susanne McConnel has twice been nominated for the Pushcart Prize and has won first prizes in the New Ohio Review Fiction Contest and Prime Number Magazine Flash Fiction Contest.</u> ** **"Kurt Vonnegut, Writing with Style"** <u>is available on **Amazon.com.**</u>

> *"How many have to die before we will give up these dangerous toys?"*
>
> **—Stephen King—**
> Iconic Author

<u>A Call to Action.</u> What can we do about it? First, we must accept our role by demanding Congress pass common-sense gun laws. Polls indicate people want them, but polls don't get the job done. **The Prevention Institute** offers some common-sense solutions.

>*Reduce easy access to dangerous weapons.
>*Establish a culture of gun

safety.

*Reduce firearm access to youth and individuals who are at risk of harming themselves or others.

*Hold the gun industry accountable and ensure adequate oversight over the marketing and sales of guns and ammunition.

*Engage responsible gun dealers and owners in solutions.

*Insist on mandatory training and licensing for owners.

*Require safe and secure gun storage.

*Remain active and let your feeling known to your elected officials.

<u>*The Prevention Institute is a non-profit organization that builds prevention and health equity into critical policies at the federal, state, and local levels to ensure that people are safe and well-being.*</u>

The **Consequences** of gun violence.

We'll wrap this up with an excerpt from the website ***everytownresearch.org***

"In an average year, gun violence in America kills nearly 40,000 people, injures more than twice as many, and costs our nation $280 billion. This staggering figure is higher than the entire US Department of Veterans Affairs' annual budget. The human cost of gun violence—the people who were taken from us and the survivors whose lives are forever altered—is the most devastating. But examining the serious economic consequences of gun violence is paramount to understanding how extensive and expensive this crisis is. And during these times of unprecedented economic uncertainty and stretched-thin health care resources from the coronavirus pandemic, these vast funds could be directed elsewhere if many of these shooting tragedies were prevented from occurring in the first place."

We can protect the 2nd Amendment and save lives lost to rising gun violence by enacting common-sense gun laws that allow Federal, State, and local authorities to keep guns out of the hands of those who should not have them. These are not arguable issues but worthy goals.

To read more, Google: **The Economic Cost of Gun Violence.**

The final word goes to Fred Guttenberg, whose daughter Jaime lost her life on February 14, 2018, at Marjory Stoneman Douglas High School in Parkland, Florida.

"My daughter Jaime was murdered in the

AMERICA

Parkland school shooting... I spend every moment thinking of my daughter and the fear that she had run from a gunman with an AR-15 at her back. Our life, which was used to revolve around her dance activities, has changed. Our days now include scheduling a visit to the cemetery. My days, which used to begin and end by greeting my daughter and telling her that I loved her, now begin and end with me crying over her loss. My evenings, which used to involve watching my favorite TV shows such as Chicago Fire and Chicago PD, are now emptier. Her friends are not having Sweet 16s, and for me, it is very hard to watch, as I will never experience that. I used to dream of her first boyfriend, first job, college, and walking her down the aisle. I miss my daughter, and it does not get easier."

Mr. Guttenberg has dedicated his life as an activist against gun violence. He has joined with **Brady**, an American nonprofit organization that advocates for gun control and against gun violence. Fred and his wife Jennifer formed ***Orange Ribbons for Jaime*** (ORFJ), a 501(c)(3), to honor their daughter by supporting causes important to her in life but also causes that deal with the way her life was tragically cut short. Learn more by following this link:
https://orangeribbonsforjaime.org/

STANDING STRONG

AMERICA

__Our World's Deteriorating Environment__

> *"When the last tree is cut, the last fish is caught, and the last river is polluted; when to breathe the air is sickening, you will realize, too late, that wealth is not in bank accounts and that you can't eat money."*
>
> ***—Alanis Obomsawin—***
> Abenaki American Canadian filmmaker, singer, artist, and activist known for her documentary films

What went wrong, and what went right.

On April 27, 2022, NOVA on PBS broadcast an episode titled, **"Can we Cool Our Planet?"** The program description read, "As global temperatures rise, scientists wonder if we need solutions beyond reducing emissions. The options may seem futuristic or challenging to implement, from sucking carbon straight out of the air, geoengineering our atmosphere, physically blocking out sunlight, and planting more than a trillion trees. But as time runs out on conventional solutions to climate change, scientists ask the hard questions: Can new, sometimes controversial, solutions really work? And at what cost?"

Let's begin with some hard facts.

The United Nations **Intergovernmental Panel on Climate Change** (IPCC) issued a recent report that pulled no punches. Unless global greenhouse gas emissions peak three years later and are cut nearly in half by 2030, the world will likely experience extreme climate impacts. Jim Skea, co-chair of the IPCC working group that produced the report, said, "It's now or never if we want to limit global warming to 1.5°C. It will be impossible without immediate and deep emissions reductions across all sectors."

Houston, we have a problem!

"The fact we are still having this discussion and, even more, that we are still supporting fossil fuels directly or indirectly using taxpayer money is a disgrace."

—*Greta Thunberg*—
Swedish environmental activist

AMERICA

If anyone doubts that immediate action is not required, consider the current events that scientists say will change life on earth for all future generations. For example, after temperatures spiked 70°F above average, the East Antarctica ice shelf collapsed and could raise global sea levels by several feet. In West Antarctica, the Thwaites ice shelf could melt in the next decade, leaving the entire glacier at risk.

So much for owning beachfront property.

Ice scientist Walt Meier told the Associated Press, "You don't see the north and the south (poles) melting simultaneously. It's definitely an unusual occurrence. It's pretty stunning."

"Wow. I have never seen anything like this in the Antarctic," said University of Colorado ice scientist Ted Scambos, who had visited the area.

"Not a good sign when you see that sort of thing happen," said University of Wisconsin meteorologist Matthew Lazzara.

The record-breaking 2020 hurricane season saw as much as 11% higher rainfall because of the human-caused climate crisis. "What that means is not only is climate change impacting our hurricane season, but it's also impacting the most extreme storms a little bit more," Kevin Reed, a climate and hurricane scientist at Stony Brook University and lead author of the study. "So, the key takeaway is that climate change is already affecting our hurricane seasons."

Ask people living across the middle states up through the Northeast what they think since experiencing extreme weather and increased tornadoes than in the past. As the saying goes, the horse is out of the barn and running free in the meadow.

> *"Every year, the problems are getting worse. We are at the limits. If I may use a strong word, I would say that we are at the limits of suicide."*
>
> **—Pope Francis—**
> Head of the Catholic Church and sovereign of the Vatican City State

We can blame the lack of transparency on the doorstep of those in authority who were warned and failed to take action or educate the public of the impending danger. This next piece of information should make everyone angry.

In the middle of a sweltering summer, James Hansen, a NASA researcher, sat

AMERICA

quietly before a Congressional committee and told them, "The greenhouse effect has been detected, and it is changing our climate now."

Hansen informed the committee that it was ninety-nine percent certain the earth was slowly turning warmer than previously measured. He said an unmistakable cause-and-effect relationship between the greenhouse effect and climate scientists reported the hottest 12-month period found by climate scientists.

Hansen's appearance before the committee was **June 23, 1988, 34 years ago.** To add injury to insult, Dr. Gavin Schmidt, director of the NASA Goddard Institute for Space Studies, stated, "There is no going back. We are reaping what we've sown."

Was Congress taking Mr. Hansen or Dr. Schmidt seriously back in 1988? Either they did not, or economic considerations took precedence, and the impending crisis was tabled. The reality is that we are now in a global foot race to take action before it is too late, and any consideration that places cost and economics ahead of action is insane. Several scientists have suggested it may be too late, and near and future generations will face as much as three times the climate challenges as their grandparents. Astounding.

Make of that what you will.

"Humanity has long since run down the clock on climate change. It's "one minute to midnight on that doomsday clock, and we need to act now."

—Boris Johnson—
Prime Minister of the United Kingdom and
Leader of the Conservative Party

In a Bloomberg.com article, *Todd Woody reported, "Around the world, millions of unsuspecting humans are breathing dirty air that far exceeds health guidelines even as climate change is making pollution worse. Sensor measurements levels of PM2.5, micrometers and smaller in length found in vehicle exhaust, power plant emissions, desert dust storms and smoke from cooking stove and wildfires."

It would serve us well if everyone read this excellent report.

<u>Todd Woody is executive editor for environment at News Deeply. Google: **These Are the Places with the Dirtiest Air in the World (and the Cleanest) to read the entire article.**</u>

AMERICA

Deep inside a mountain on a remote island in the remote Svalbard archipelago, halfway between mainland Norway and the North Pole, lies the Global Seed Vault Seed bank, which opened in 2008. The Vault is one of over 1000 gene-seed banks around the globe now storing duplicates of seed samples from the world's crops. Why? In anticipation of a possible worldwide catastrophe. Could the catastrophe be severe climate change that brings about a worldwide food shortage? Considering how much talk we've heard about the difficulty of feeding the world's growing population, we should be very, very concerned. As food-growing areas are affected by extreme heat and no rain, turning them into dust fields, a severe worldwide food shortage could cause millions to die.

"Every once in a while, I feel despair over the fate of the planet. If you've been following climate science, you know what I mean: the sense that we're hurtling toward catastrophe, but nobody wants to hear about it or do anything to avert it."

—*Paul Krugman*—
Nobel Memorial Prize Winner in Economic Sciences

STANDING STRONG

Have you heard about the ***Earth's Black Box**? No? You're not going to like what you read, but here goes.

The Earth's Black Box is a bus-sized piece of equipment being built in the Tasmanian desert with only one purpose—to record all data on the climate crisis. An article in ***ecowatch.com*** explains how the Black Box will continuously collect data for analysis. The project's website tells us, "The device's purpose is to provide an unbiased account of the events that lead to the planet's demise, hold accountability for future generations, and inspire urgent action. How the story ends is completely up to us. Only one thing is certain, your actions, inactions, and interactions are now being recorded."

Pretty frightening to think that we would require such a device to let us know whether or not humanity has a decent chance of survival. The article on the Earth's Black Box is yet another must-read.

To read the article, Google: ***Earth's Black Box Will Tell Future Generations the Story of the Climate Crisis.***

AMERICA

"Please make no mistake— climate change is the biggest threat to security that modern humans have ever faced... There is no going back - no matter what we do now, it's too late to avoid climate change and the poorest, the most vulnerable, those with the least security, are now certain to suffer... If we bring emissions down with sufficient vigor, we may yet avoid the tipping points that will make runaway climate change unstoppable."

—*Sir David Attenborough*—
English broadcaster, natural historian, and author

In her article for **NewRepublic.com**, *Liza Featherstone wrote: "A recent landmark study of young people all over the world showed how widespread this question is. Thirty-nine percent of the young people surveyed said they are hesitant to have children of their own because of the climate crisis. The concern is greater in some countries: 47 percent are reluctant to have kids in the climate-vulnerable Philippines and 48 percent in Brazil, where Jair

STANDING STRONG

Bolsonaro's far-right government has presided over unprecedented deforestation of the Amazon rain forest, the world's biggest carbon sink."

If we hope to keep the human race going, common-sense climate policies must be passed. Read Lisa Featherston's article to hear the words of the young forced to deal with the mess we're leaving behind.

Liza Featherstone teaches "Writing on Policy" at SIPA and is the advice columnist for The Nation, where she is a contributing editor. To read the entire article, Google: **If Politicians Want to Raise Birth Rates, They Should Pass Climate Policy.** *Her new book,* **"Divining Desire: Focus Groups and the Culture of Consultation,"** *is available on* **Amazon.com**.

> "We, the human species, are confronting a planetary emergency... the earth has a fever. And the fever is rising... Indeed, without realizing it, we have begun to wage war on the earth itself."
>
> **—Albert Arnold Gore Jr.—**
> 45th vice president of the United States

In 2021, the COP26 climate change conference sent a strong signal regarding what amounted to an apocalypse if we don't act on the climate crisis now. But in direct conflict with that statement, agreements are coming slowly. As reported in the ***Hill.com**, at the end of 2021, governments worldwide find themselves on a tightrope. The deals reached suggested the world could move to avoid the worst near-term doomsday scenarios. Despite U.S. climate envoy John Kerry's call for action, the international commitments to fossil fuels remain unshaken, "We are closer than we have ever been before to avoiding climate chaos and securing cleaner air, safer water, and a healthier planet."

To read the article, Google:
Equilibrium/Sustainability — Dam failures cap a year of disasters.

> *"If you want to understand the opposition to climate action, follow the money."*
>
> **—Paul Krugman—**
> Nobel Memorial Prize Winner in
> Economic Sciences

One way or the other, it always comes down to *Follow the Money.*

Every one of us has a role to play. Start

with this list of organizations that we can join and support. Through them, we are not a single voice but part of a chorus of voices all working to the same end—our species' current and future survival.

350. org
https://350.org/
Citizens Climate Lobby
https://citizensclimatelobby.org/
Climate Reality Project
https://www.climaterealityproject.org/
Climate Solutions
https://www.climatesolutions.org/
ConservAmerica
https://www.conservamerica.org/
Earth Justice
https://earthjustice.org/
ecoAmerica
https://ecoamerica.org/
Greenpeace USA
https://www.greenpeace.org/usa/

We adults should follow the younger generation's example. They are taking action through ***Our Children's Trust***, a non-profit public interest law firm right here in America. The organization presents solutions. The website is worth visiting to see how everyone can participate in this vital movement.

Learn more at: **www.ourchildrenstrust.org.**

AMERICA

"The one good thing about science is that it's true whether or not you believe in it."

—*Neil deGrasse Tyson*—
American Astrophysicist

Who are we saving it for if we're not taking action to save the planet for ourselves and future societies? That's the critical question each of us is called upon to answer before one day, not too far off in the future; Mankind will have left Planet Earth to the bugs and animals, who may or may not be the only ones to survive.

The future, as we say, belongs to the young. They face a tough road ahead in dealing with climate change's real-life threat to humanity.

Here are the angry voices of two young women majoring in environmental studies at Eckerd College in St. Petersburg, Florida. Hopefully, they will go on in their careers to help solve one of the most urgent issues that, if not solved, could one day mark the end of the human race as we know it.

STANDING STRONG

"The younger generation is almost put on a pedestal to save the planet. It's like, we didn't create this problem.

—*Anya Cervantes*—
Environmentalist, artist, photographer

"It's going to be a painful ending, and it's going to happen in an unjust way."

—*Anna Lyn Heine*—

<u>**A Call to Action.** We can make our voices heard by</u> writing elected officials at the state and federal levels to ensure that whatever solutions are available are being implemented to control further climate change damage. We cannot assume that federal and state governments are placing climate change ahead of concerns over the economy. It always comes down to money. But not this time because we cannot afford to wait. We have been living on the planet and doing our best to destroy it.

<u>*For suggestions on what we as individuals can do to protect ourselves and all future generations, Google:* **7 ways to get proactive about climate change instead of feeling helpless: Lessons from a leadership expert.**</u>

AMERICA

<u>The **Consequences** to the humans from climate change:</u>

> *Wildfires, floods, and droughts.
> *Extreme heat waves.
> *More intense & violent storms.
> *Rising sea levels.
> *Melting glaciers.
> *Water shortages caused by droughts causing food shortages.
> *The loss of animals and plants and human life.
> *Continued damage to homes & property.
> *Higher electric bills & more blackouts.
> *More allergies & other vital health risks.

STANDING STRONG

The final word goes to Leonardo DiCaprio.

"This is not a partisan debate; it is a human one. Clean air and water and a livable climate are our inalienable human rights. And solving this crisis is not a question of politics. It is our moral obligation."

—Leonardo DiCaprio—
American actor, Film Producer & Environmental Activist

AMERICA

The 2020 Pandemic

> *"Everyone has something to contribute. Wear a mask, keep social distancing, and if you have the possibility to get vaccinated, just do it. Do it for yourself and for your loved ones. And that's how we can all do our bit to end this pandemic."*
>
> **—*Justin Trudeau*—**
> Prime Minister of Canada

What went wrong, and what went right.

The following belongs in **Ripley's Believe It or Not**... or at least an episode of the **Twilight Zone**.

Nostradamus, French astrologer, physician, and reputed seer of future events, predicted the following in the year 1551: "There will be a twin year (2020) from which will arise a queen (corona) who will come from the east (China) and who will spread a plague (virus) in the darkness of night, on a country with seven hills (Italy) and will transform the twilight of men into dust (death), to destroy and ruin the world. It will be the end of the world economy as you know it."

Make of that what you will. Now for some disturbing news.

On May 7th, ***The Washington Post*** reported that the Biden administration is warning the United States could see 100 million coronavirus infections and a potentially significant wave of deaths this fall and winter, driven by new omicron subvariants that have shown a remarkable ability to escape immunity... Several experts agreed that a major wave this fall and winter is possible, given waning immunity from vaccines and infections, loosened restrictions, and the rise of variants better able to escape immune protections. Many have warned that returning to more relaxed behaviors, from going maskless to participating in crowded indoor social gatherings, would lead to more infections. The seven-day national average of new infections more than doubled from 29,312 on March 30, 2021 to nearly 71,000 Friday (May 6), a little more than five weeks later... Natalie Dean, a biostatistician at Emory University, said the longer the time period between coronavirus waves, the greater the number of people who will be vulnerable to infection because of waning immunity. "That just puts vulnerable people back at risk," Dean said. "It seems likely there will continue to be these ups and downs."

To read Yasmeen Abutaleb and Joel Achenbach's article, Google: **Coronavirus wave this fall could infect 100 million, administration warns**

Let us pause and recall the spouses, parents, siblings, and children who have already lost loved ones as we move on.

We need to understand what went wrong and what went right with the pandemic. To begin with, we are an impatient species, always looking for the easiest way out of any dilemma. In the case of the pandemic, as thousands began to get sick and die, we quickly learned there was going to be no easy way out. Those who refused the vaccine claimed personal choice or called it a hoax or an unproven and dangerous vaccine. It turned out to be just the opposite; it has saved lives.

By the middle of April 2022, worldwide, there were 6,260,020 cases of COVID-19 reported, with 6.19 million deaths and climbing. However, the World Health Organization says the coronavirus pandemic led to nearly 15 million excess deaths worldwide. We may never know the exact number.

By early May of 2022, over 81 million patients and 1 million deaths were reported in the United States. That is more than living in the cities of Las Vegas, Detroit, Portland, Memphis, Louisville, Milwaukee, Baltimore, Albuquerque, Atlanta, Kansas City, Raleigh, Omaha, and Miami and more than the lives lost in the Civil War. Sadly, we can anticipate the number of deaths in the U.S. to reach one million-plus. However, with the data that confirms vaccinations have proven successful in reducing the severity, hospitalizations, and deaths, it is difficult to understand why approximately 33% still refuse to get vaccinated. Freedom to make one's own decisions is one thing, but when those decisions affect others, the decision must be for the good of all.

In her book, **American Pandemic: The Lost Worlds of the 1918 Influenza Epidemic,** *Nancy Bristow writes that while going back to a pre-pandemic normal may be appealing, history shows it could have harmful implications both for this pandemic as well as the next one. "That drive to not have to do what we've been doing carries with it a great potential to forget," she says. "How Americans continue to think that these kinds of things won't happen to us, that kind of

American exceptionalism. You can only do that if you are a nation that is very, very capable of forgetting moments of its past."

**Nancy K. Bristow is a Professor of History at the University of Puget Sound in Tacoma, Washington, and the author of: "Making Men Moral: Social Engineering during the Great War, and the American Pandemic," available at Amazon.com.*
*Emily Martin is a professor of socio-cultural anthropology at New York University. To read more, Google: **The lessons learned from 1918 flu fatigue to explore this subject further.***

As it always does, it comes down to history and education and why we repeat the same mistakes from generation to generation. The 1918 Influenza Epidemic is a perfect example; in 2020, we made some of the same mistakes people made back in 1918.

STANDING STRONG

> *"For me, the biggest casualty of the pandemic is trust in science. The rapid development of the vaccine saved millions of lives. But 40% of Americans believe the nonsense about the vaccine and the coronavirus, including its origin, treatment, and damage to the human body from Covid-19. We have a lot of work to do to overcome that blow to science. The health and safety of our children and grandchildren depend on scientific progress, and it is up to us to defend science and scientists if we hope to prevent future catastrophes."*

—*Robert Hubbell*—
Publisher of Today's Edition Newsletter at:
roberthubble@substack.com

Consider that if a foreign enemy had invaded America, we would have come together as true patriots to protect our country. And yet, we were invaded by a foreign entity, one we could not see but was a mass killer just the same. The burning question of why some choose not to join the fight to curb the spread of the virus will shadow us for generations to come.

To explore this phenomenon further, read Geoff Brumfiel's article. Google: ***Vaccine Refusal May Put Herd Immunity at Risk, Researchers Warn.*** *Brumfiel is a senior editor and correspondent on* ***NPR's*** *science desk.*

> *"If you don't want to wear a mask or get vaccinated, you are really gonna' hate having a respirator tube down your throat and wearing diapers."*
>
> **—*Mia Farrow*—**
> American actress and activist

Despite the flow of misinformation initially coming from the White House, it was another story behind the scenes. On May 15, 2020, at the urging of medical experts, the White House announced the authorization of **Operation Warp Speed**, which made it possible for the medical community and pharmaceutical companies to create and make available a vaccine in record time. For this, the former administration deserves full credit. But the early public misstatements made by the former administration led to an endless flow of conspiracy theories and misinformation causing confusion and apprehension among the general public. Then, the Federal Government passed off responsibility for controlling the virus to the ill-prepared States. It was like tossing the problem to 50 individual countries and hoping for the best results.

The public was not made aware, for example, of the 20 years or so of scientific and medical studies that had taken place, making it possible for the COVID-19 vaccine to become available as quickly as it did. If shared with the public, that information would have added validity and earlier compliance by the people, which could have saved lives. Instead, conspiracy theories and misinformation left many believing it was fake news or medical quackery. We've heard numerous stories from those who chose not to get vaccinated only to contract COVID and recant while on ventilators.

Thankfully, the battle cry from those whose life work was to protect public health remained constant.

> *"Even though you may not get any symptoms, what you're doing is that you're propagating the outbreak. You will almost certainly, or one of your colleagues will infect someone else, who will infect someone else, who will infect somebody who really, really, gets sick,"*

—*Dr. Anthony Fauci*—
Physician-scientist and immunologist serving as the director of the National Institute of Allergy and Infectious Diseases and the Chief Medical Advisor to the President

Do we need to be reminded that it is the government's job to protect us against such national emergencies? Conspiracy theories and misinformation aside, the government made it possible to create and distribute the vaccine in record time, which has saved many lives.

"I would say what I'm bothered by most is that hundreds of thousands of Americans died unnecessarily. It's a terrible waste of life and didn't have to be that way. We're having such a terrible response and an inability to implement basic public health measures... If we'd done a lockdown better across the country, we could have lower transmission rates and then open things up much easier. But ... we didn't."

—Dr. Ezekiel Emanuel—
Former White House health adviser – Chairs the Department of Medical Ethics and Health Policy at the University of Pennsylvania

Snake oil charlatans and scammers came out of the woodwork and profited by peddling drugs like hydroxychloroquine. Anti-vaccine Facebook groups posted notes telling people to stay away from hospitals and try dangerous at-home treatments instead. It was sheer madness that fueled fear amongst the tribes.

There was yet another downside to the pandemic. We may never appreciate the toll it took on the medical community, those professionals who worked tirelessly and who paid a personal price to save lives. Here as we go forward, are some of their voices.

> *"I've never seen doctors, nurses, and hospital staff so sad. Literally all of them. Like they're losing a war, and they've just now realized it."*

—Brian, MD—
@bone00afide

> *"Certain moments trigger something that makes me really sad. I can be at home and be totally fine, and at bedtime, all of a sudden, sobs and anxiety kick in."*

—Brittani Holsbeke—
Nurse, Beaumont Hospital, Farmington Hills, Michigan

STANDING STRONG

"Everything was happening so quickly. Everyone was dying so quickly. We had to go from one death to another and the next. I was imagining it happening to my family and being in a situation like that."

—Marc Ayoub, MD—
Resident, NYC Health – Elmhurst Hospital

*"This will be my most sincere Tweet ever. I am pleading with everyone who will listen. I'm so tired. We're all so tired. And we're running out of resources and people.
Please...please help us."*

—That Liberal Nurse—
@Abn_RN

If asked, these comments would be consistent with every doctor, nurse, and medical assistant who cared for and continue to care for COVID patients.

In isolation and on a ventilator, Nic Brown fought for his life against the coronavirus. The medical intensive care unit (MICU) staff at Cleveland Clinic used the one window in his room to post uplifting messages. "Every day I was there," Mr. Brown said, "especially when I was on a ventilator and full life support, the staff would write on the window the goals for me to try and reach each day. They would encourage me. One day someone wrote, *'We will get you home.'*"

When Nic was well enough to go home, he left a message on that window. "I watched you work hard to keep me and others alive, unable to thank you for the time that you poured into me — and although I will probably never get the chance to pour that same love and support into you, I want you to know that I think you all are rockstars." Later, when he was home again, Nic said, "Part of why I left the note on the window is because I don't know that I've ever seen such selfless people in my life. I really saw the love of God through them. They didn't know me, but they cared for me like I was a member of their family. It's been life-altering."

Medical professionals return to work each day because that is what they are trained for, and they do it well, returning each day to their workplaces that resemble war zones. We owe them our thanks. We owe them our lives.

Now, from the sublime to the ridiculous.

"I had an unvaccinated person tell me yesterday that he didn't believe that 800,00 people have died of Covid in the US – and that they (authorities) are putting that on death certificates to make it look worse than it is. How do you respond to such nonsense?

—AnniezOpz—
@Laiebchbum

The answer to Anniez's question is that we must try to impart truth, facts, and common sense to those who have been misled.

There is more disturbing news coming from the medical community as they begin studying how neurological problems from COVID-19 cause patients long-term problems like brain fog, anxiety, and depression, trouble thinking, among other reported symptoms.

According to a new study conducted in the United Kingdom and published online in the journal ***eClinicalMedicine***, people who require hospitalization for COVID-19 develop lingering cognitive problems similar to what you'd expect if they'd aged 20 years. The research is limited because it included fewer than 50 COVID-19 patients. Still, it adds to the ample research that suggests that the coronavirus infection leaves a lasting impact on the brain in ways yet understood.

We'll be hearing a lot more about these COVID after-effects throughout the rest of 2022 and beyond.

BA.2m, a new omicron subvariant of the virus, is the most recent concern of infections spreading across the globe, and no one knows for sure if there will be even more variants. The unvaccinated accounted for the overwhelming majority of deaths in the United States from the pandemic. But that has since changed according to a Washington Post analysis of state and federal data.

The pandemic's toll is no longer falling exclusively on those who chose not to get shots, with vaccine protection waning over time and the elderly and immunocompromised at greatest risk of succumbing to covid-19, even if vaccinated — having a more challenging time dodging increasingly contagious strains.

To read Fenit Nirappil and Dan Keating's Washington Post article, Google: **Covid deaths no longer overwhelmingly among unvaccinated as toll on elderly grows.**

A Call to Action. How our response to the pandemic went wrong, and how can we fight the next virus challenge. The answer is quite simple. We can listen to medical professionals and trust science. We call a plumber, not an electrician when we need a plumber. The analogy applies here.

The **Consequences** of the pandemic are many:

*Covid destroyed many careers, leaving economic distress in its wake.
*Many families find themselves on food stamps for the first time.
*Patients who survive COVID suffer from debilitating exhaustion and pain for months.
*Gun violence during the pandemic rose by 30%, and anger and incivility rose to new levels. How was either supposed to help?
*During the pandemic, America's drug overdose epidemic grew worse.
*Suicide rates increased during the pandemic.
*Missing regular in-person schooling has caused children to experience stress and emotional problems leaving many at risk of dropping out.
*Higher proportions of

AMERICA

Americans between ages 13 and 24 say the pandemic has made their education, career goals, and social lives more difficult than millennials and Gen X.

*There has been an accelerated mental health crisis reported among adolescents. More than 4 in 10 teens report that they feel "persistently sad or hopeless," and 1 in 5 say they have contemplated suicide.

*Teacher stress spiked amid substitute shortages and added responsibilities. Many have quit the profession. Stress scores were highest among nursing assistants, medical assistants, social workers, and inpatient workers, and many quit their profession.

*The global supply chain system broke down and led to inflation, leading to a new high in the cost of living.

*In the U.S., gun violence was up over previous years.

* The virus can disrupt smell and taste and how humans perceive the world. For some, the losses may be permanent.

STANDING STRONG

The final word on this subject goes to Neil DeGrasse Tyson.

> *"The problem in society is not kids not knowing science. The problem is adults not knowing science. They outnumber kids 5 to 1, they wield power, and they write legislation. When you have scientifically illiterate adults, you have undermined the very fabric of what makes a nation wealthy and strong."*

—*Neil deGrasse Tyson*—
American Astrophysicist

AMERICA

Black Lives Matter: The Movement

"If I would have just not taken the bill, this could have been avoided."

—Christopher Martin—
The store clerk who accused George Floyd of passing a fake $20 bill

What went wrong, and what went right?

On May 25th, Mr. Martin called the police. When they arrived, angry words were exchanged. Mr. Floyd was handcuffed and placed face down in the road. Police Officer Derek Chauvin then pressed his knee into the back of Floyd's neck for 9 minutes and 29 seconds. At least 28 times, Mr. Floyd said, *"I can't breathe,"* as well as *"Help me"* and *"Mama."*

It was all caught on a nearby witness's cellphone and later broadcast.

Mr. Floyd was pronounced dead at 9:25 PM. The county medical examiner ruled the death a homicide caused by the officer's use of force, fentanyl, and methamphetamine in Mr. Floyd's system and Floyd's other underlying health conditions. He was 46 years old.

The video of Floyd's and Chauvin's encounter spurred nationwide peaceful protests against police brutality and systemic racism. And yet, as always, some ruined it for the rest by inciting violence, looting, and destruction of personal property. In at least 21 cities National Guard was activated, removing protestors with tear gas and rubber bullets.

On April 20, Derek Chauvin, 45, was found guilty of second-degree murder, third-degree murder, and second-degree manslaughter and sentenced to 22.5 years.

"Today, we are able to breathe again."

—Philonise Floyd—
Brother of George Floyd

Many assume that George Floyd's tragic death was the beginning of the Black Lives Matter movement. It was not.

First, some stats from **Pew Research Center**. About six-in-ten Americans (58%)

say race relations in the U.S. are wrong, and of those, few see them improving. Some 56% think the former president made race relations worse; just 15% say he has improved race relations, and another 13% say he failed to progress this issue. In addition, roughly two-thirds say it's become more common for some to express racist views after the former president was elected.

Make of that what you will. Three steps forward, two back.

Now to the Black Lives Matter Movement and its beginnings. The following is from ***blacklivesmatter.com.***

In 2013, three Black organizers — Alicia Garza, Patrisse Cullors, and Opal Tometi — created a Black-centered political will and movement building project called **#*BlackLivesMatter*.** It was in response to the acquittal of Trayvon Martin's murderer George Zimmerman on February 26, 2012. The project is now a member-led global network of more than 40 chapters. Our members organize and build local power to intervene in violence inflicted on Black communities by the state and vigilantes.

Black Lives Matter is an ideological and political intervention in a world where Black lives are systematically and intentionally targeted for demise. It is an affirmation of

Black folks' humanity, our contributions to this society, and our resilience in the face of deadly oppression. Soon we created the Black Lives Matter Global Network infrastructure. It is adaptive and decentralized, with a set of guiding principles. Our goal is to support the development of new Black leaders, as well as create a network where Black people feel empowered to determine our destinies in our communities.

> *"We need the harm to stop in our communities. We need the damage to be repaired. We need to be able to have the opportunity to have a life of dignity and the possibility to thrive."*
>
> **—Opal Tometi—**
> Co-founder, Black Lives Matter movement

"Each time I look at America's government pinnacles — the Capitol, the White House, and National Mall monuments — I am reminded of the Black men whose hands built those magnificent structures and the perilous conditions under which they worked: their bodies used as human ladders; their comrades lost and buried below. A nation built by Black men and boys should protect Black men and boys," said Representative Frederica S. Wilson of Florida in her opinion piece for ***TheHill.com.**

To read the entire article, Google: **2022: The year of Black men.**

> "Ultimately, when our responses become human responses as opposed to racial responses, that is when we're going to change as a society."
>
> ***—Dr. Finnie Coleman—***
> University of New Mexico Associate Professor

"Ideas that come into the public consciousness during protest do not simply disappear," reports **TheConversion.com**. "They stick around. We found that six months after the 2020 George Floyd protests, social media searches of terms such as systemic racism and white supremacy were considerably higher than before the protests.

Black Lives Matter demonstrations were a regular occurrence in the U.S. between 2014 and the end of 2020. Still, some periods saw significantly more public participation in marches and demonstrations in communities across the country. At key moments, often after the death of another Black man at the hands of the police, large groups were in the streets. At those times, more people conducted online searches for the term "Black Lives Matter," showing that the public protests did indeed generate wider awareness of the movement's events and issues... The trend continued as time passed. In December 2020, #BlackLivesMatter tweets were posted about 10,000 times per day, compared with fewer than 1,000 for **#AllLivesMatter** or **#BlueLivesMatter**. The data suggests that the Black Lives Matter movement has a lasting impact – as are the group's ideas."

<u>Article authored by Jelani Ince, Assistant Professor of Sociology, University of Washington, and Zackary Dunivin, Ph.D. Student in Sociology and Complex Systems, Indiana University. To read the article, Google: **Black Lives Matter protests are shaping how people understand racial inequality.**</u>

Although there has been significant progress, much more work remains.

A Call to Action. <u>What can we do to improve racial relations?</u>

> *Talk to our family members – there is nothing funny about racism.

*Be introspective.
*Avoid stereotypical language.
*Try teaching through examples.
*Step out of your comfort zone. The time has come to move beyond our biases.
*Know thyself. If you're not part of the solution, you're part of the problem.

Source: Charles A. Gallagher. To read more, Google: ***Ten Things You Can Do to Improve Race Relations.***

The **Consequences** of racism.

*Racial discrimination is a critical social determinant of health and a driver of racial & ethnic health inequities.

*Racism fosters hate which can lead to discriminatory violence.

*Racism is in direct conflict with the Constitution and the values it purports to defend on behalf of all citizens.

*Racism neither serves nor advances society. It is just the opposite; it holds us back in many ways.

The final word goes to President Barack Obama.

STANDING STRONG

"It's important for us to also understand that the phrase, 'Black Lives Matter' simply refers to the notion that there's a specific vulnerability for African Americans that need to be addressed. It's meant to suggest that other lives don't matter. It's to suggest that other folks aren't experiencing this particular vulnerability."

—*Barack Obama*—
44th President of the United States

AMERICA

The 2020 Election

"It has been said that politics is the second oldest profession. I have learned that it bears a striking resemblance to the first."

—*Ronald Reagan*—
(1911 – 2004)
40th President of the United States

What went wrong, what went right.

Despite the former President's continued insistence that the 2020 election was rigged, election officials unanimously confirmed it was one of the most secure. But what occurred next raised serious questions about why so many were willing to accept false information at face value. Why have many in Congress continued to fuel the fire by publicly supporting lies and misinformation?

You can't make this stuff up. Read on.

In 2022 U.S. District Judge David Carter ruled that the former president of the United States "likely attempted to obstruct the joint session of Congress" by his attempts to convince Vice President Mike Pence he had the authority to determine the results of the 2020 election. "The illegality of the plan was obvious," Judge Carter wrote. "Dr. [John] Eastman and President Trump launched a campaign to overturn a democratic election, an action unprecedented in American history. Their campaign was not confined to the ivory tower — it was a coup in search of a legal theory. Every American — and certainly the president of the United States — knows that in a democracy, leaders are elected, not installed. With a plan this 'BOLD,' President Trump knowingly tried to subvert this fundamental principle... This evidence demonstrates that President Trump likely knew the electoral count plan had no factual justification... Based on the evidence, the Court finds it more likely than not that President Trump corruptly attempted to obstruct the joint session of Congress on January 6, 2021... If Dr. Eastman and President Trump's plan had worked, it would have permanently ended the peaceful transition of power, undermining American democracy and the Constitution."

"Par-dessus tout," French for *"Above All Else."* Our Constitution is to be protected and upheld *"above all else."*

If Mike Pence had followed the illegal

maneuvers presented, the government would have found itself in political and legal chaos from which it may have never recovered. Everything this country and the American people once stood for could have been stripped away.

We have to think long and hard about the next time an unqualified politician—a wolf in sheep's clothing—comes along promising what they cannot deliver. Proven integrity, morals, and qualifications are the only criteria for choosing to give our support to a candidate. Too many do not to follow this simple logic.

Let's examine some of the familiar bad actors behind the drama that could have led to our government being stolen: The former president, attorney John Eastman, attorney Rudy Giuliani, Chief of Staff Mark Meadows, Political gangster Roger Stone, political insider Dan Scavino, former advisors to the President Peter Navarro, and Steve Bannon, attorney Sidney Powell, former National Security Advisor Mike Flynn, MyPillow CEO Mike Lindell, and Ginni Thomas, the wife of Supreme Court Justice Clarence Thomas. These good folks will have a special place in history reserved just for them.

Who besides these well-known names might be involved? Who provided the funding for this effort? What is painfully slow in coming are the names of the members of Congress who had a hand in this notorious affair. Why? Hopefully, the January 6th investigation committee will spotlight each in their upcoming public hearings.

Presidential Advisor Peter Navarro willingly revealed his role in an interview with MSNBC'S Ari Melber and *Jose Pagliery of **TheDailyBeast.com**. In his published memoir, Navarro detailed how he stayed in close contact with Trump advisor Steve Bannon as they put in motion a plan with the support of the former president and members of Congress who were supposedly loyal to him. An argument might be that some— if not all—are not dedicated to the former president but how it might advance them, or those citizens who continue to support the "Big Lie," knowing there are votes to be mined within that group in the next election. That's the hypocrisy of politics and politicians.

Mr. Navarro admitted to Mr. Pagliery that he and Bannon were behind the last-ditch coordinated effort to keep the former president in power. They dubbed the plan the **'Green Bay Sweep.'** "We spent a lot of time lining up over 100 congressmen, including some senators," Navarro stated. "It started out perfectly. At 1 p.m., (Paul) Gosar and (Ted) Cruz did exactly what was expected of them... We didn't even need any protestors because we had over 100 congressmen committed to it."

Mr. Navarro was charged with contempt of Congress for ignoring a subpoena. Jail time, anyone?

Before we return to Mr. Pagliery's article, let us take note that one hundred duly elected members of Congress expressed their support of a plan that, if successful, would have overturned the will of the American people. They placed their hand on the Bible and took an oath of office. Have they no integrity, no moral obligation to uphold the United States Constitution? Those proven to be involved should be removed from Congress and labeled "Benedick Arnold's," who, during the Revolutionary War of 1780, was an American military officer who defected to the British side of the conflict. Whether they stay or go will be up to the voters.

In his article, Mr. Pagliery reported: "The plan had little or no chance <u>of decertifying the election results on its own</u>, a point that Navarro acknowledged. The hope was to run the clock as long as possible to increase public pressure on then-Vice President Mike Pence to send the electoral votes back to six contested states. Republican-led legislatures would attempt to overturn the election results. Ramping up pressure on Pence would require media coverage. "Steve Bannon's role was to figure out how to use this information—what he called 'receipts'—to overturn the election result," Navarro said. "That's how Steve had come up with the *Green Bay Sweep* idea."

Later that same day, Bannon referenced the football-themed *Green Bay Sweep* strategy on his daily podcast, the **War Room Pandemic**.

Jose Pagliery is a political investigations reporter at The Daily Beast. To read the article, Google: ***Trump Adviser Peter Navarro Lays Out How He and Bannon Planned to Overturn Biden's Electoral Win.***

Then there's Ginni Thomas, wife of Supreme Court Justice Clarence Thomas, well known for her off-the-wall right-wing activity. The January 6th committee has revealed her string of text messengers to Chief of Staff Mark Meadows. It appears she encouraged Meadows "to keep the president on track to take whatever steps necessary to remain in office." She shared with Mark Meadows conspiracy theories like this one that read like it was happening in real-time. "Biden crime family & ballot fraud co-conspirators (elected officials, bureaucrats, social media censorship mongers, fake stream media reporters, etc.) are being arrested & detained for ballot fraud right now & over coming days, & will be living in barges off GITMO to face military tribunals for sedition."

What in the world was she smoking?

Mrs. Thomas urged that the president "not concede" because "it takes time for the army who is gathering for his back." What did she mean by "an army gathering for his back?" Was it to be a protest or another armed insurrection?

Another text to Meadows referenced conversations that she'd had with 'Jared.' "Just forwarded to your Gmail," she wrote, "an email I sent Jared this am... Help This Great President stand firm, Mark!!! ... You are the leader, with him, who is standing for America's constitutional governance at the precipice. The majority knows Biden and the Left are attempting the greatest heist of our history."

On November 5, 2020, as first reported by CNN, Donald Trump Jr. texted Mark Meadows outlining ways to keep his father in office. "We have operational control," Trump Jr. told Meadows. "We have multiple paths. We control them all." Trump Jr. outlined a plan involving lawsuits and recounts in swing states and alternative slates of "Trump electors." If that failed, Trump Jr. suggested Congress could instead vote to reinstall

Trump on Jan. 6, 2021.

Proof that the apple doesn't fall far from the tree.

The investigation committee is revealing more and more information: more names, more texts, more everything that will undoubtedly lead to charges and possible prosecution.

As for the now-infamous "Eastman Memo," that' s like Emperor Julius Caesar's advisors sending him a last-minute memo telling him that maybe their advice to cross the Rubicon was a bad idea. Too late, Caesar and his army were already wading across the Rubicon to begin the Roman Civil War. Ops!

Make of that what you will.

The rule of law must now apply to anyone found guilty as it did to the eleven men sentenced to prison for their involvement in President Richard Nixon's Watergate scandal. Nixon was allowed to resign and live out his life in peace as a civilian—which begs the question: will the former president be prosecuted if found guilty of criminal doing?

AMERICA

"The political lesson of Watergate is this: Never again must America allow an arrogant, elite guard of political adolescents to by-pass the regular party organization and dictate the terms of a national election."

—Gerald R. Ford—
(1913 – 2006)
38th president of the United States

The Congressional committee investigating the January 6 insurrection confirmed that as the poll closed, a data expert working for the former president informed him it looked like he would lose. Bill Barr, the U.S. Attorney General, confirmed the DOJ had found no evidence of a fraudulent election. All states certified their elections. Yet, the former president has yet to accept or acknowledge his loss and continues to privately and publicly insist there was massive voter fraud when there was none.

Blind ambition trumps morality every time.

STANDING STRONG

"The ignorance of one voter in a democracy impairs the security of all."

—John F. Kennedy—
35th President of the United States

Even though the former president lost, supporters of the "Big Lie" posted on Facebook some 650,000 posts attacking the legitimacy of the election. It began in earnest on election day and continued through January 6th. You can't make this stuff up. "Looks like civil war is becoming inevitable!!!" read a Facebook post a month before the Capitol assault. "We cannot allow fraudulent elections to stand! Silent no more, the majority must rise up now and demand battleground states not to certify fraudulent elections now!" Yet another post showed an avatar of a smiling woman with her arms raised in apparent triumph that read, "We are Americans!!! We fought and died to start our country! We are going to fight... fight like hell. We will save her, then were going to shoot the traitors!!!!!!!!!!" Yet another post pictured a Civil War-era picture of gallows. Waiting was a couple of dozen hooded figures as if they were about to be hanged. Hard to believe, but others posted calling for the arrests and executions of some Democrats and Republicans who stood in the way of a second term for the former president.

It's a challenge to understand the thought process of people who would post this trash. And yet, they cannot be discarded as bad or evil people because most of them, if not all, are not. They are our relatives, neighbors, and people who work in and serve our communities. It behooves us to understand why they took the stance they did and engage them in sensible dialogue that leads to the truth, not lies, misinformation, or conspiracy theories. That is a tall order indeed.

> *"Voter fraud is a reality in American elections, but it is typical of the candidate to confuse the anecdote with data and turn allegations into conspiracies."*
>
> **—Bret Stephens—**
> Pulitzer Prize-winning American conservative journalist, Opinion columnist for The New York Times & Senior contributor to NBC News

With no hard evidence to support his claims, the former president, never one to give in, took his "Big Lie" to the courts. Sixty-three courts, including the Supreme Court, turned him away.

But that's not where this Twilight Zone fantasy ends.

While the former president was on the phone telling Georgia Secretary of State Brad Raffensperger, "All I want to do is this: I just want to find 11,780 votes, which is one more than we have... Fellas, I need 11,000 votes, give me a break,"—his lieutenants were gathered in a suite at the posh Willard Hotel just down the street from the White House. There, they conjured up plans to keep the former president in office. Present were Rudolph W. Giuliani, Stephen K. Bannon, Bernard Kerik, former New York City police commissioner, and John Eastman of the infamous "Eastman Memo."

<u>Note: **"The Eastman Memo"** is reprinted at the end of this book.</u>

Regarding that now-infamous Eastman Memo, here for everyone's enlightenment are emails between John Eastman and Mike Pence's top lawyer while the insurrection mob made their way into the Capital. Most people are not aware of these back-and-forth conversations.

Pence's attorney to Eastman: "I have run down every legal trail placed before me to its conclusion, and I respectfully conclude that as a legal framework, it is a results-oriented position that you would never support if attempted by the opposition, and essentially entirely made up... And thanks to your bullshit, we are now under siege."

Eastman shot back: "The 'siege' is because you and your boss did not do what was necessary to allow this to be aired in a public way so the American people can see for themselves what happened."

Pence's attorney to Eastman: The advice provided has, whether intended or not, functioned as a serpent in the ear of the President of the United States, the most powerful office in the entire world. And here we are... respectfully, it was gravely, gravely irresponsible for you to entice the President with an academic theory that had no legal viability and that you well know we would lose before any judge who heard and decided the case. And if the courts declined to hear it, I suppose it could only be decided in the streets. The knowing amplification of that theory through numerous surrogates, whipping large numbers of people into a frenzy over something with no chance of ever attaining legal force through the actual process of law, has led us to where we are."

There you have it in black and white. It

was an attempt to overturn the will of American voters and install a gang of political hacks who were ready to go to any lengths to hold onto political power and control over the country's future—and a zigzag future it will have been.

> *"Here in America, we are descended in blood and in spirit from revolutionists and rebels - men and women who dare to dissent from accepted doctrine. As their heirs, may we never confuse honest dissent with disloyal subversion."*
>
> **—*Dwight D. Eisenhower*—**
> (1890 – 1969)
> 34th President of the United States

As if the Eastman memo wasn't bizarre enough, a second memo, written by campaign attorney Jenna Ellis, targeted the counting of electoral votes. If VP Mike Pence followed instructions, the House could choose the next president using fraudulent alternative electors.

Guess who that next President would have been?

AMERICA

"Freedom only survives if we protect it. We must speak the truth. The election was not stolen. America has not failed."

—Liz Cheney—
Member of United States House of Representatives

If only the madness had ended there, but it did not. This group kept tossing stuff against the wall, hoping something would stick, even encouraging the President to invoke Martial Law. When that didn't happen, what they came up with next was worthy of an Oscar © in the category of "Worst Movie Plot."

CNN reported two drafts of an executive order drawn up to seize voting machines—one directed the Department of Defense to get it done and another to the Department of Homeland Security. Think about that for a moment. What would they do with those machines if they had got their hands on them?

A copy of this executive order is reproduced at the end of this book. It reads like a Tom Clancy political suspense thriller, only not nearly as well written.

STANDING STRONG

To read Reporters Zachary Cohen and Paula Reid's CNN article, Google: ***Exclusive: Trump advisers drafted more than one executive order to seize voting machines, sources tell CNN.***

> *"There are people in every time and every land who want to stop history in its tracks... they fear the future, mistrust the present and invoke the security of a comfortable past, which in fact, never existed."*

—Robert F. Kennedy—
(1925 – 1968)
American lawyer and politician & 64th United States Attorney General

February 1, 2022. The former president wasn't done with Mike Pence. He urged Congressional investigators to investigate why Pence did not reject electoral college votes of some of the states won by Joe Biden.

In a speech at a Federalist Society in Florida, Vice President Pence rebuked the president with these words: "There are those in our party who believe that as the presiding officer over the joint session of Congress, I possessed unilateral authority to reject Electoral College votes. And I heard this week that President Trump said I had the right to 'overturn the election. President Trump is wrong. I had no right to overturn the election." The former vice president added, "The presidency <u>belongs to the American people, and the American people alone.</u> Frankly, there is almost no idea more un-American than the notion that any one person could choose the American president."

The former president wasted no time in firing back. "Just saw Mike Pence's statement on the fact that he had no right to do anything concerning the Electoral Vote Count, other than being an automatic conveyor belt for the Old Crow Mitch McConnell to get Biden elected President as quickly as possible... Well, the Vice President's position is not an automatic conveyor if obvious signs of voter fraud or irregularities exist."

Keep saying it repeatedly, and eventually, many will believe it.

This entire misadventure should teach us that no one man or group can ever be allowed to attempt to overturn the will of the American people for personal political gains. That is what dictators do. Ensuring that this never happens again is the responsibility of every American citizen, including the disgruntled.

A Call to Action. What can we do about this failed attack on American democracy? The answer always remains the same: First, put party affiliation and religious and personal beliefs aside long enough to know all we can about the background, qualification, integrity, and morality of the candidate we choose to back. Listen carefully to their words and understand their meaning because they can often be misleading. And most importantly, show up to vote on election day and vote with our heads and not our hearts. The future of America counts on it.

The **Consequences** resulting from the 2020 election.

>*If overturning a legitimate election had succeeded, Americans could live under the beginning of a disguised autocracy.
>*Laws are being changed to make it difficult for certain people to vote in the very near future.
>*The rule of law could become ancient history.
>*America's standing and influence in the world have been damaged.

AMERICA

*Finally, we ran the risk of losing everything we now hold dear.

The final word goes to Alexander Hamilton.

"This process of election affords a moral certainty that the office of President will seldom fall to the lot of any man who is not in an eminent degree endowed with the requisite qualifications."

—*Alexander Hamilton*—
(Died: July 12, 1804)
American statesman & one of the
Founding Fathers of the United States

To prepare for the next section, please take a moment to read the following.

18 U.S. Code § 2385. Advocating the overthrow of the Government

Whoever knowingly or willfully advocates, abets, advises, or teaches the duty, necessity, desirability, or propriety of overthrowing or destroying the government of the United States or the government of any State, Territory, District or Possession thereof, or the government of any political subdivision therein, by force or violence, or by the assassination of any officer of any such government; or... Whoever, with intent to cause the overthrow or destruction of any such government, prints, publishes, edits, issues, circulates, sells, distributes, or publicly displays any written or printed matter advocating, advising, or teaching the duty, necessity, desirability, or propriety of overthrowing or destroying any government in the United States by force or violence, or attempts to do so; or... Whoever organizes or helps or attempts to organize any society, group, or assembly of persons who teach, advocate, or encourage the overthrow or destruction of any such government by force or violence; or becomes or is a member of, or affiliates with, any such society, group, or assembly of persons, knowing the purposes thereof—Shall be fined under this title or imprisoned not more than twenty years, or both, and shall be ineligible for employment by the United States or any department or agency thereof, for the five years next following his conviction. If two or

AMERICA

more persons conspire to commit any offense named in this section, each shall be fined under this title or imprisoned not more than twenty years, or both, and shall be ineligible for employment by the United States or any department or agency thereof, for the five years next following his conviction. As used in this section, the terms "organizes" and "organize" with respect to any society, group, or assembly of persons, including the recruiting of new members, the forming of new units, and the regrouping or expansion of existing clubs, classes, and other units of such society, group, or assembly of persons.

STANDING STRONG

January 6, 2021

"Today is a reminder, a painful one, that democracy is fragile. To preserve it requires people of good will, leaders with the courage to stand up, who are devoted not to the pursuit of power and personal interest at any cost, but the common good."

—Joe R. Biden—
At the time, he was President-Elect

What went wrong, and what went right?

As more text and phone messages are revealed, they confirm January 6 was not spontaneous but premeditated by high-ranking government officials and outside groups to overturn the legitimate results of the 2020 election to keep the former president in office.

As reported by **CBS News**, William Todd Wilson of North Carolina admitted joining other Oath Keepers, including leader Stewart

Rhodes, to use force to halt the peaceful transfer of power from then-President Donald Trump to President Joe Biden. Wilson admitted under oath to a Statement of Offense, which is used in criminal proceedings to stipulate the facts of the case that a defendant acknowledges.

"At approximately 5:00 p.m., Wilson, Rhodes, and others left the Capitol grounds and walked together to the Phoenix Hotel," the statement read. "Rhodes then called an individual over speaker phone. Wilson heard Rhodes repeatedly implore the individual to tell President Trump to call upon groups like the Oath Keepers to oppose the transfer of power forcibly."

The allegation is the first time a member of Oath Keepers, charged with the most severe crimes surrounding the January 6 attack, is accused of attempting to contact Trump on January 6. Rhodes allegedly implored the group in one "Leadership" group, "We aren't getting through this without a civil war. Too late for that. Prepare your mind, body, spirit."

Wilson admitted to bringing an AR- 15-style rifle, a 9-millimeter pistol, approximately 200 rounds of ammunition, body armor, a camouflaged combat uniform, pepper spray, a large walking stick intended for use as a weapon, and a pocketknife to a

Washington, D.C.-area hotel room ahead of the attack. Wilson "heard Rhodes discuss the potential need for Rhodes and co-conspirators to engage in force, up to and including lethal violence, to stop the transfer of power."

There we have it; what occurred was carefully planned and coordinated in advance.

Robert Legare is an Associate Producer at CBS News. To read the article, Google: **Oath Keepers leader Stewart Rhodes tried to contact Trump during the January 6 Capitol attack, court documents reveal.**

And the horror began. In bewildered silence, we watched the mob head to the Capitol following weeks of the former president making the false claim that the election was rigged and that he had won "BIG!" How could this be happening in the United States of America? It was the kind of lunacy we expect from *tyrants* in third-world countries.

Washington Post reporters Carol D. Leunig and Phil Rucker wrote in their book, "I Alone Can Fix It," that Gen. Mark A. Milley, chairman of the Joint Chiefs of Staff, was so concerned about the threat of a coup attempt by Trump and his allies, that he discussed a plan with his fellow joint chiefs to resign rather than carry out orders from Trump that they viewed as illegal. General Milley, who was concerned about Trump's rash of personnel moves after the election, "told his staff that he believed Trump was stoking unrest, possibly in hopes of an excuse to invoke the Insurrection Act and call out the military."

Now, that's as close to frightening as any of us want to get.

<u>To read the article, Google:</u> **Talk of martial law, Insurrection Act draws notice of Jan. 6 committee.** <u>Carol D. Leonnig and Phil Rucker's book,</u> **"I Alone Can Fix It,"** <u>is available on</u> **Amazon.com.**

"The cost of freedom is always high, but Americans have always paid it. And one path we shall never choose, and that is the path of surrender and submission."

—John F. Kennedy—
(1917 – 1961)
35th President of the United States

University of Northern Colorado Professor of History Fritz Fischer, Ph.D., offered common-sense context from a historical perspective. "What happened on January 6 was an unprecedented insurrection; it was a riot, and it's debatable whether we can call it a coup, but it resembled a coup... The reason we are so shocked and appalled is that what happened has never really happened before." Professor Fischer added, "The riot itself wasn't the most shocking thing; the most shocking thing was that it was <u>our own president</u> who directed an attack on our Congress, and that has no precedent in U.S. history and surprisingly few in world history. To have one part of our government attack another part of the government is insane, and it was dangerous and antithetical to any traditional understanding of how our government should work."

<u>*To read Professor Fischer's article, Google:* **UNC Expert: The Capitol Riot and its Lasting Impacts.**</u>

"There is no grievance that is a fit object of redress by mob law."

—*Abraham Lincoln*—
(1809 – 1864)
16th President of the United States

"When law ends, tyranny begins."

—*John Locke*—
(1632 – 1704)
English philosopher & physician - an influential

of Enlightenment thinkers known
as the "Father of Liberalism."

Out of public view, what was going on confirms the invasion was organized with precision in advance by ambitious political hacks hell-bent on keeping power. Power, after all, is a potent aphrodisiac.

> *"It was democracy itself, not simply the Capitol, that was under siege. People who faithfully remember Independence Day should never forget the day that our Capitol—the people's House — was taken over by an angry mob."*
>
> ***—Brad Bannon—***
> Opinion Contributor for TheHill.com

For clarity, it is essential to revisit the timeline leading up to January 6th. On December 19, 2019, one week before Christmas, the former president of the United States Tweeted: "Big protest in D.C. on January 6th. Be there; it will be wild!" On December 26th, he Tweeted: "See you in Washington, DC, on January 6th. Don't miss it. Information to follow." On January 1st:

STANDING STRONG

"The BIG Protest Rally in Washington, D.C. will take place at 11:00 A.M. on January 6th. Locational details to follow."

What did the former president know that we didn't?

Then, on January 5th, 2021, Steve Bannon, former advisor to the former president, announced on his radio show: "All Hell is going to take place tomorrow."

Was Bannon's message the final signal that the invasion was a "go?"

Read on, and you decide.

The crowd that had traveled to Washington gathered on the Ellipse to listen to fiery speeches meant to fire them up. The so-called "Patriots" cheered on as attorney Rudy Giuliani spoke on the Ellipse. "He (Pence) can decide on the validity of these crooked ballots," Giuliani told the crowd. "Or he can send it back to the legislators and give them five to ten days to finish the work. We now have letters from five legislators begging us to do that. They're asking us—Georgia, Pennsylvania, Arizona, Wisconsin, and one other coming in." He also told the crowd, "Let's have trial by combat."

Like lemmings cheering on the Pied Piper, the unruly crowd roared: "Rudy, Rudy, Rudy, Rudy."

In his trademark Panama hat, the author

of the infamous 'Eastman Memo,' John Eastman told the gathering, "We know there was fraud... dead people voted... voting machines contained a secret folder of ballots, challenging the very essence of our republican form of government. All we are demanding of Vice President Pence is this afternoon at one o'clock, he let the legislatures of the states look into this so that we get to the bottom of it and the American people know whether we have control of the direction of our government or not! We no longer live in a self-governing republic if we can't get the answer to this question!"

Note: One week later, Eastman was forced to resign from Chapman University after students and colleagues accused him of helping incite the riot in the Capital.

U.S. Representative Mo Brooks of Alabama, whose reputation for making outlandish political statements proceeded him, roared at the top of his voice: "Start taking down names and kicking ass... Our ancestors sacrificed their blood, their sweat, their tears, their fortunes, and sometimes their lives. Are you willing to do the same? Are you willing to do what it takes to fight for America? Carry the message to Capitol Hill... the fight begins today."

This is the same Mo Brooks who later said: "The President made me do it." Google it. Giuliani, Eastman, and Brooks had only one job; whip the crowd into a frenzy for the final act.

Finally, the president approached the podium and began to speak. He whipped up the crowd as only he could. "All of us here today do not want to see our election victory stolen by emboldened radical Democrats... We will never give up. We will never concede. It will never happen. You don't concede when there's theft involved. Our country has had enough. We will not take it anymore. We fight like hell. And if you don't fight like hell, you're not going to have a country anymore. So, we're going to... we're going to walk down Pennsylvania Avenue. I love Pennsylvania Avenue. And we're going to the Capitol, and we're going to try and give... *(note the pause like he was about to say something he should not on an open mike)*. "So, let's walk down Pennsylvania Avenue."

Banana Republic, anyone?

> *"What really was under attack on Jan. 6th was the cornerstone of our democracy, which is free and fair elections."*
>
> **—Barbara F. Walter—**
> Political science professor, University of California at San Diego & a Central

AMERICA

Intelligence Agency advisor

The organization known as the **Oath Keepers**, who claim the federal government is part of an evil conspiracy intent on stripping Americans of their natural rights and freedoms, were the primary organizers behind the insurrection and a group called Proud Boys.

Reporter Samantha Putterman of ***PolitiFact.com*** provided a precise recreation of the events documenting how well planned and organized the insurgents were. "Of the more than 600 charged in connection with the Jan. 6 insurrection, no one was more coordinated in their efforts to disrupt the congressional certification of the U.S. electoral votes than these individuals. They prepared themselves for battle, equipped with communication devices and various tactical items, including vests, helmets, ballistic goggles, and hard-knuckle gloves. They were known as the **Oath Keepers**. Among their members were active-duty military, veterans, and some with law enforcement experience who joined the organization since its founding in 2009. The group's motto, "Not on our watch," emphasized a level of vigilance against a perceived threat that could strike at any time... In the words of one Oath Keeper affiliate, "This is everything we f—king trained for."

To read Samantha Putterman's article for PolitiFact, Google: **_Everything we trained for': How the far-right Oath Keepers militia planned for violence on Jan. 6th_**

"We're in! We're in! We're in! We're in! Derrick Evans is in the Capitol!" a voice yelled over communications. Derrick Evans was a newly elected Republican member of the West Virginia House of Delegates running with the insurgents. What the hell was he doing running with the insurgents? His constituents will have to answer that question.

Two sources who were part of the planning—both have been granted anonymity due to an ongoing investigation—described how they participated in "dozens" of planning briefings with Republican Congressional members and officials within the administration. The two men have named names. Read Hunter Walker's Rolling Stone article to find out who they identified.

To read the article, Goggle: **_EXCLUSIVE: Jan. 6 Protest Organizers Say They Participated in 'Dozens' of Planning Meetings with Members of Congress and White House Staff._**

A reporter on the scene questioned one of the rioters about their goal. The man's chilling answer was: "The people in this house, who stole this election from us, hanging from gallows out here on this lawn for the whole world to see, so it never happens again. That's what needs to happen. Four by four by four, hanging from a rope out here for treason."

It is beyond belief that anyone of sound mind would make such a hideous statement. Would the insurrectionists have gone through with their threats if they could have?

> *"The best way of dealing with the few slackers or trouble makers in our midst is first, to shame them by patriotic example, and, if that fails, to use the sovereignty of government to save the government."*
>
> **—*Franklin D. Roosevelt—***
> (1882 – 1945)
> 32nd President of the United States

Once he was made aware of what was happening outside, Vice-President Pence called acting defense secretary Christopher Miller and ordered him to "Clear the Capital!"

It didn't happen. Why?

STANDING STRONG

From inside the Capital, Congressional members were making calls. "I am in the House Chambers," Representative Dan Kildee said, "We have been instructed to lie down on the floor and put on our gas masks. Chamber security and Capitol Police have their guns drawn as protesters bang on the front door of the chamber. This is not a protest. This is an attack on America."

An hour after the Senate Chamber had been breached, House Majority Leader Chuck Schumer called the Army to deploy the National Guard, pleading, "We need help!"

In a call with Pentagon leaders, chairman of the Joint Chiefs, Mark Milley said: "We must establish order."

Help did not arrive. Why? Did the president use his authority as Commander in Chief to put the brakes on these requests? A question in search of an answer that may never be answered.

> *"This is how election results are disputed in a banana republic... I am appalled by the reckless behavior of some political leaders since the election and by the lack of respect shown today for our institutions, our traditions, and our law enforcement."*

AMERICA

—George W. Bush—
43rd President of the United States

Tammy Patrick, the former elections official in Arizona's Maricopa County, said, "If no one is held responsible for lying ... or undermining confidence based on their greed and, you know, desire for power to either be elected or be reelected — if no one is held accountable for those actions, then we are in real trouble right now."

The Justice Department has since unsealed seditious conspiracy charges against Oath Keepers leader Stewart Rhodes and ten others, alleging they plotted to disrupt the electoral process at the U.S. Capitol on Jan. 6 and endangered former Vice President Mike Pence and others.

> *"Those who can make you believe absurdities can make you commit atrocities."*

—Voltaire—
(1694 – 1778)
François-Marie Arouet, known by his nom de plume Voltaire, was a French Enlightenment writer, historian, & philosopher

STANDING STRONG

When it was over, and Vice President Mike Pence failed to do what was demanded of him, the sitting president of the United States took to his favorite public platform and tweeted: "Mike Pence didn't have the courage to do what should have been done to protect our country and our Constitution, giving States a chance to certify a corrected set of facts, not the fraudulent or inaccurate ones they were asked to previously certified. The USA demands the truth!"

Mr. former president, you can't handle the truth.

> *"History will rightly remember today's violence at the Capitol, incited by a sitting president who has continued to baselessly lie about the outcome of a lawful election, as a moment of great dishonor and shame for our nation."*
>
> **—*President Barack Obama*—**
> 44th President of the United States

As the January 6 Committee continues to investigate, the question remains, who besides the president and his gang of hangers-on were behind this heinous act, and who financed it.

Who, what, where, how, and why?

Following the attack, the former president's message to the January 6th crowd remained the same: "These are the things and events that happen when a sacred landslide election victory is so unceremoniously & viciously stripped away from great patriots who have been badly & unfairly treated for so long. Go home with love & in peace. Remember this day forever!"

Yes, the American people will remember that day forever, Mr. President, but not how you had hoped.

We know the rest. The angry, violent, white supremacist mob, carrying both American and Confederate flags, stormed the U.S. Capital, injured 140 Capital Police, and did physical damage to areas of the Capital.

Police Officer Brian Sicknick died the day after being overpowered and beaten by the mob. Following the attack, four other officers died by suicide: Officer Gunther Hashida, Officer Kyle DeFreytag, Jeffrey Smith, and Officer Howard Liebengood. Four people who were part of the mob died: Ashli Babbitt, who a Capital Police Office shot, and Kevin D. Greeson, Rosanne Boyland, and Benjamin Philips by other causes.

Another issue that has been made public

is why internal White House records from January 6 show a gaping hole in the presidential phone logs. Seven hours and 37 minutes were missing, some while the Capital building was being invaded. White House staffers have already established that the president used other phones to make calls not entered on the daily log.

Since the end of March 2022, over 800 have been charged for their participation in the insurrection, and most await trial. Many have pleaded guilty, throwing themselves at the mercy of the courts. Many, if not all, wish they had stayed home and not bought into the big lie from the man who presently continues to roam free in his expansive mansion in sunny South Florida.

In January of 2022, at a gathering in Texas, the former president stated that if reelected in 2024, he intended to pardon any insurrectionist charged. "If I run and if I win, we will treat those people from January 6 fairly. And if it requires pardons, we will give the pardons. They are being treated so unfairly."

That flies in the face of his previous statement that, "To those who engage in acts of violence and destruction, you do not represent our country. And to those who broke the law, you will pay."

AMERICA

Pour yourself a stiff drink and make of that what you will.

> *"The American people deserve the full and open testimony of every person with knowledge of the planning and preparation for January 6th."*

—Elizabeth Lynne Cheney—
United States Representative from Arizona.

Here is an excerpt from Chairman Bennie Thompson when on July 27, 2021, he opened the U.S. House Select Committee investigating January 6th:

"We won victories, and we've suffered failures, but the peaceful transfer of power has stood as the pillar of our democracy... We can rest easy knowing that when the moment comes, our system guarantees that one party will hand the reigns to another if that's the will of the people. And while our institutions endured and while Joe Biden is the legitimately elected President of the United States, a peaceful transfer of power didn't happen this year. It did not happen. Let that sink in. Think about it. A violent mob was pointed toward the Capitol and told to win a trial by combat."

To read the entire transcript, Google: **Rep. Bennie Thompson Opening Statement Transcript: House Investigation of January 6.**

Robert B. Hubbel, the publisher of Today's Edition Newsletter, wraps up this chapter with words we should all take to heart. "If we do not proclaim the true lesson of January 6th, others will fill the void with conspiracies and disinformation and false grievances. Do not let them do so. Do not give them space, do not afford them legitimacy in the name of civility, and do not let them forget that they are traitors to the Constitution. Unless we speak plainly about what happened on January 6th, unless we claim that day for ourselves, we may not be ready to respond if others try again. The true lesson of January 6th is that the Constitution is ours only so long as we are prepared to defend it in word and deed."

Subscribe to "Today's Edition Newsletter: at: **roberthubbell.substack.com/**

> *"January 6th wasn't a peaceful protest. It wasn't a riot. It was an insurrection meant to overthrow the electoral process and install Donald Trump as an American dictator."*

AMERICA

—*Stephen King*—
Iconic Author

Dustin Thompson, a 38-year-old exterminator from Ohio, who took part in invading the Capital, told Judge Reggie Walton, "Besides being ordered by the President to go to the Capitol, I don't know what I was thinking. I was caught up in the moment... If the President is giving you almost an order to do something, I felt obligated to do that,"

As he sent Thompson immediately to jail pending sentencing, Walton said, "You make your bed, you lie in it." Thompson then took off his tie, belt, and jacket and was handcuffed behind his back by a deputy US marshal and escorted out of the courtroom.

Call to action. To avoid another January 6, we must first show our support as the investigation goes forward and accept nothing less than the prosecution of those involved to the full extent of the law. In doing so, we stand the best chance of avoiding another January 6. Congress has a responsibility to pass legislation that ensures the peaceful transfer of presidential power. Beyond these steps, common-sense thinking must rule. Don't believe everything you hear because in politics, what you hear can be coming from wolves disguised in sheep's clothing.

The **Consequences** of the January 6th insurrection.

*Some continue to deny, minimize, or normalize the legacy of the attempted coup dividing the country even more than it already is.

*The attack depleted citizens' confidence in the election process.

*The Capital riots revealed U.S. democracy's vulnerability.

*The attack was well planned, and our security agencies missed the signals.

*The realization of how vulnerable the U.S. can be to domestic terrorism. Terrorists is what the insurrectionists were, not patriots but domestic terrorists.

*The threat that it could happen again is enough to engage all of the above.

The final word goes to President John F. Kennedy.

AMERICA

"For in a government of laws and not of men, no man, however prominent or powerful, and no mob, however unruly or boisterous is entitled to defy a court of law. If this country should ever reach the point where any man or group of men by force or threat of force could long defy the commands of our courts and our constitution, then no law would stand free from doubt, no judge would be sure of his writ, and no citizen would be safe from his neighbors."

—*John F. Kennedy*—
(1917 – 1963)
35th President of the United States

Conspiracy Theories & Misinformation

"When we hear new information, we often think about what it may mean. If we later hear a correction, it doesn't invalidate our thoughts—and it's our own thoughts that can maintain a bias, even when we accept that the original information was false."

—Norbert Schwarz, Ph.D.—
Psychology Professor, University of Southern California

What went wrong, and what went right.

Trust but verify, because truth matters. We live in a message swamp where daily stuff is just made up, and truth and facts be damned if they get in the way of greed and ambition. It has become so bad that no one knows who or what to believe.

Here is a perfect example.

AMERICA

"Devil, your foot soldiers are coming out tonight. They're coming all the way out. We will expel them," Pastor Greg Locke of Mt. Juliet, Tennessee, howled from the stage in a crowded white tent. "You gotta leave, Devil," he shouted, "you gotta get out!"

Wielding a microphone as he paced the stage, his wife, Tai, at his side, Locke called out, "spirits of anger, rage, bitterness, lust, and envy. Spirit of molestation, spirit of abuse, get out right now!" Locke commanded. "Every spirit of homosexuality, lesbianism, come out, come out," his wife ordered. "Transgenderism, gender dysphoria, come out. We rebuke it. We rebuke it!" Locke yelled.

As reported by Annie Gowen in the Washington Post, the tent slowly took on a spirit of its own. Worshipers began writhing as if in pain. Others waved their hands in the air in benediction. "Amens" began to mix with the guttural sound of growling, moaning, and praying in tongues.

"If you've had a covid-19 shot, I'm telling you you've got poison in your veins," Locke thundered. "We call out the covid-19 vaccine out right now. Keep that demonic spirit out of you right now in the name of Jesus!"

<u>Annie Gowen is a correspondent for The Post's National desk. To read the article, Google:</u> **<u>A Jan. 6 pastor divides his Tennessee community with</u>**

increasingly extremist views to read the entire article.

Pastor Locke, who is head of the Global Vision Bible Church, gained national attention when he kept his church open and defied the mask mandates of the "fake pandemic." Why would he mislead millions of his followers? A better question might be, why do his followers believe such blatant misinformation that may have caused many of them to end up in a hospital on ventilators?

> *"The truth may be puzzling. It may take some work to grapple with. It may be counterintuitive. It may contradict deeply held prejudices. It may not be consonant with what we desperately want to be true. But our preferences do not determine what's true."*
>
> **—*Carl Sagan*—**
> (1934 – 1996)
> Astronomer, planetary scientist, cosmologist, astrophysicist, astrobiologist, author, & Science communicator

AMERICA

Endless conspiracy theories and misinformation is spread around like manure. Call it what it is: 1st Amendment abuse and information corruption readily accepted at face value by many who then pass it on as fact. As Charles Darwin warned us in **The Descent of Man**, "Ignorance more frequently begets confidence than knowledge."

New research by Josh Hart, associate professor of psychology, suggests in the **Journal of Individual Differences** that people with certain personality traits and cognitive styles are more likely to believe in conspiracy theories. "These people tend to be more suspicious, untrusting, eccentric, needing to feel special, with a tendency to regard the world as an inherently dangerous place," Hart said. "They are also more likely to detect meaningful patterns where they might not exist. People who are reluctant to believe in conspiracy theories tend to have the opposite qualities."

Josh J. Hart is a professor in the *Psychology department at Union College, Barbourville, Kentucky. To read the article, Google:* **Who believes in conspiracies? New research offers a theory.**

STANDING STRONG

"Some voters live in a so-called populist bubble where they hear nationalist and xenophobic messages, learn to distrust fact-based media and evidence-based science, and become receptive to conspiracy theories and suspicious of democratic institutions.

—Anne Applebaum—
Polish-American Pulitzer Prize journalist & historian - Staff Writer at The Atlantic, Washington Post columnist and former of the editorial board

Incredibly immoral is the misinformation spread by political candidates and elected officials seeking political advantage, which has become the new normal in today's hyper-political environment. Some statements are just plain dumb when spoken in the moment; others are carefully crafted to skirt the line of truth just enough to sow doubt, knowing some will believe the worst.

A disturbing report from the University of Chicago says that 19% of Americans believe the government was behind the 9/11 attacks, 25% believe the 2008 recession was caused by a small cabal of Wall Street Bankers, and 11% believe the government-mandated a switch to compact fluorescent lightbulbs in government buildings because they make people obedient and easier to control.

I would have chosen the fake Moon landing myself.

"Sometimes people don't want to hear the truth because they don't want their illusions destroyed."

—*Friedrich Nietzsche*—
(1844 – 1900)
German philosopher, cultural critic,
composer, poet, writer

Have you heard of **The International Flat Earth Society**? It was founded in the 1950s by one Samuel Shenton with a membership roster that reached as many as 3500. Since the earth was flat, they believed sunrises and sunsets had to be an optical illusion. Neither could a flat-earth be orbited, making the Space Shuttle a big hoax. Ironically, Mr. Shenton lived a stone's throw from Edwards Air Force Base in southern California, where the Space Shuttles landed after their return to Earth. Is there no end to ignorance?

Make of that what you will.

STANDING STRONG

"The search for truth takes you where the evidence leads you, even if, at first, you don't want to go there.

—*Bart Denton Ehrman*—
American New Testament scholar

But wait, it gets even nuttier.

A ***YouTube*** conspiracy channel shared a 22-minute video that falsely claimed George Floyd was alive and police officer Derek Chauvin was an actor. The "deep state," whoever they are, orchestrated the entire incident.

Another conspiracy theory that's been around for a while claims that the U.S. Government is out to get us, which is illogical when we think about it. The U.S. Government —although it often acts like it—is not a separate entity; <u>it is us, the American people.</u> Read the bloody Constitution already. It states that <u>we, the people are in charge,</u> not our employees inside the beltway in that shining city on the hill we call Washington.

Is it any wonder why fake news actually reaches more people and spreads more quickly than the truth? Who doesn't like a bit of juicy misinformation or made-up conspiracy theory?

AMERICA

A study by Dartmouth University computer scientist Soroush Vosoughi, Ph.D., and colleagues reported: "Fake news has important implications in politics, but also in areas such as health and nutrition, climate science, and financial information," says David Rand, Ph.D., a professor of management science and brain and cognitive sciences at MIT. "The basic question from a psychological perspective is: How can people possibly believe this stuff?"

How indeed?

"If you want to assert a truth, first, make sure it's not just an opinion that you desperately want to be true."

—Neil deGrasse Tyson—
American astrophysicist

The late Carl Sagan said, "Extraordinary claims require extraordinary evidence." Add to that the words of former Secretary of Defense James Schlesinger: "Everyone is entitled to his own opinion, but not his own facts."

STANDING STRONG

"It isn't what we don't know that gives us trouble, it's what we know that ain't so.

—Will Rogers—
(1879 – 1935)
Actor, Cowboy, Humorist, Columnist & Social Commentator

Let's examine a few of the better-known spreaders of information trash. To introduce us to the granddaddy of them all, we turn to journalist *Adrienne LaFrance.

"If you were an adherent, no one would be able to tell. You would look like any other American. You could be a mother, picking leftovers off your toddler's plate. You could be the young man in headphones across the street. You could be a bookkeeper, a dentist, or a grandmother icing a few cupcakes in her kitchen," LaFrance writes. "You may well have an affiliation with an evangelical church. But you are hard to identify just from the way you look—which is good because someday soon, dark forces may try to track you down. You understand this sounds crazy, but you don't care." She makes the point that sums up this entire chapter. "You know that a small group of manipulators, operating in the shadows, pull the planet's strings. You know that they are powerful enough to abuse children without fear of retribution. You know that the mainstream media are their handmaidens, in partnership with Hillary Clinton and the secretive denizens of the deep state. You know that only Donald Trump stands between you and a damned and ravaged world. You see plague and pestilence sweeping the planet and understand that they are part of the plan. You know that a clash between good and evil cannot be avoided, and you yearn for the Great Awakening that is coming. And so, you must be on guard at all times. You must shield your ears from the scorn of the ignorant. You must find those who are like you. And you must be prepared to fight... You know all this because you believe in "Q."

*Adrienne LaFrance is an American journalist and executive editor of The Atlantic.com. To read the article, Google: **The Prophecies of Q.**

"Q," of course, is QAnon, which began spreading trash talk on the imageboard **8chan** owned and operated by Ron Watkins and his father, Jim. Ron and Jim posted lurid stories of child pornography and white supremacy and the dubious wisdom of someone called "Q," who, according to this site, was a high-up government official who held Q-level clearance, whatever the hell that is. Mr. "Q's" wisdom became known as "Q drops" or "breadcrumbs."

One in five Americans claims to be QAnon believers. We suspect some follow QAnon for the entertainment value.

QAnon claimed that a group of Satan-loving political bigshots was running—*wait for it, wait for it*— a child sex ring that became known as the **"Pizzagate"** scandal. This pepperoni conspiracy raised its ugly head when the email account of John Podesta, Hillary Clinton's campaign chairman, was hacked and smeared online by good old reliable WikiLeaks. QAnon claimed—without proof—Podesta's emails were actually coded messages confirming that Democratic Party bigshots were running a child sex ring. One location identified was in the basement of **Comet Ping Pong Pizzeria** in Washington, D.C. This off-the-wall fairy tale was spread across social media sites 4chan, 8chan, and Twitter.

Here is where it gets scary.

An outraged QAnon believer from North Carolina traveled to Comet Ping Pong Pizza armed with his trusty rifle. Entering the restaurant, he shot the lock off a door believed led to the cellar where the children were being held. When he pried the door open, he found a small storage room. Comet Ping Pong Pizza didn't have a basement. Who would have guessed?

That was the end of the great ***Pizzagate*** conspiracy.

And yet, some persist in believing this ludicrous story. Some elected officials continue to use "Pedophiles" in public in some political circles. We know they know better, but they are willing to put integrity aside to play to their base if they hope to keep collecting those big-government salaries and perks.

Can we apply a little common sense here? If there were a shred of proof, the media would have blown it wide open for all the world to see. Since QAnon has failed to offer any evidence, why would anyone continue to believe in this madness?

It's not surprising to learn that Ron Watkins has filed papers to <u>run for Congress in 2022,</u> representing sunny Arizona as a super conservative.

Go ahead, make of that what you will.

And then there's David Todeschini. This guy hosts a podcast as David Trent and spreads conspiracy theories about how the Democrat Party is full of pedophiles.

Todeschini told his audience, "This is proven beyond a reasonable doubt and to a moral certainty with physical, irrefutable evidence," but he neglected to provide proof.

On May 19, 1999, Mr. Todeschini was convicted of sexual abuse in the first degree and sodomy in the second degree for coercing an 8-year-old boy into sexual activity. He received a five-year prison sentence. We are left to wonder what his faithful listeners thought when they learned of that?

As for QAnon, in July 2020, Twitter banned 7,000 QAnon-linked accounts. TikTok banned QAnon-related hashtags that same month, followed by a Facebook ban in August. In October, Twitter and Facebook increased their moderation of sites like QAnon, as did YouTube.

Some individuals who have publicly voiced their support for QAnon are planning to run for the United States Congress in the 2022 midterm elections. Thirteen are from Florida, nine are from California, six from Texas, four from Illinois, three each from New York, New Jersey, and Arizona, two each from Nevada, Pennsylvania, Maryland, Tennessee, Oregon, and Ohio, and one each from Rhode Island, Virginia, North Carolina, Vermont, Iowa, Alaska, Georgia, and Colorado. The list is continually updated.

Each voter has the moral obligation to question whether these individuals are suitable for high public office.

For the names of those running as of the end of April

*2022 on the **Media Matters for America** website, Google: **Here are the QAnon supporters running for Congress in 2022.***

> *"All humans make mistakes. But there is no room or allowance in the fevered world of conspiracy theorists for mistakes, human errors, anomalies, or plain incompetence, though the latter, from the highest levels on down are endemic to our society.*
>
> **—Vincent T. Bugliosi, Jr.—**
> (1934 – 2015)
> American attorney & New York Times bestselling author

And then there's master conspiracy misinformation spreader Alex Jones, who promotes himself as a right-wing radio host and anti-government conspiracy theorist specialist, whatever that is. Mr. Jones made headlines with the ridiculous claim that the Sandy Hook elementary school massacre was a hoax staged by the U.S. government as a way to kill the 2nd Amendment. Mr. Jones also claimed the little juice boxes that kids love could make them gay, autism is caused by vaccines, and the U.S. government staged

STANDING STRONG

the 9/11 attack on the World Trade Center.

What?

Ah, but wait, there's more. While the coronavirus erupted across the country, Jones was raking in millions by peddling products and dietary supplements, referring to them as *preventative treatments* for the coronavirus. "This stuff kills the whole **sars-corona** family at point-blank range," Jones claimed. "It kills every virus."

Really, at point-blank range?

Facebook, YouTube, and Twitter have since removed Jones' trash. Apple removed Jones' Infowars store app from its App Store, but not before Jones collected an estimated 165 million dollars over a three-period from his loyal but very naïve followers.

With that kind of loose change, Mr. Jones' can easily afford his mental health expenses, or maybe not. His website, Infowars, has filed for bankruptcy because of lawsuits filed against him over his Sandy Hook conspiracy claims. Now Jones, realizing how much trouble he is in, has offered to chat with federal prosecutors about Jan. 6 in exchange for immunity against prosecution.

Portions of the above are from ***Fighting Hate for Good*** *(ADL). Google:* ***Alex Jones: Five Things to Know.***

AMERICA

"The lowest form of popular culture – lack of information, misinformation, disinformation, and a contempt for the truth or the reality of most people's lives – has overrun real journalism. Today, ordinary Americans are being stuffed with garbage.

—Carl Bernstein—
Investigative journalist & bestselling author

On his Spotify podcast, podcaster Joe Rogan told his listeners, "I'm not going to get vaccinated. I have antibodies. It doesn't make any sense... If you're like 21 years old, and you say to me, should I get vaccinated? I'll go, no." Then, in September 2021, he tested positive for COVID. "I immediately threw the kitchen sink at it by taking Ivermectin."

More dangerous information from Mr. Rogan: The FDA approved Ivermectin to treat people and animals suffering from intestinal strongyloidiasis and onchocerciasis from conditions caused by parasitic worms. The FDA warned of possible side effects, including nausea, vomiting, abdominal pain, neurologic disorders, and potentially severe hepatitis requiring hospitalization. And yet, Mr. Rogan was telling his listeners how it cured him, and some believed.

Let's not forget Joseph Mercola, who spread misleading anti-vaccine gibberish like this: The unvaccinated might soon find themselves behind bars in some government-run prison. Major media platforms have since shut down Mr. Mercola. But that hasn't stopped Mr. Mercola. Now he is spewing his garbage on **Substack**, a subscription-based newsletter platform.

Where there's a will to spread junk to willing believers, there's always a way.

Rogan, Jones, and Mercola are just three examples of those with high profiles and large numbers of followers peddling misinformation and profiting from it. They're just a few examples of the dozens and dozens out there doing the same.

"I'm not upset that you lied to me; I'm upset that from now on, I can't believe you."

—Friedrich Nietzsche—
(1844 – 1900)
German philosopher, cultural critic, composer, poet, writer

We should not demonize people who

accept what they read or hear at face value. On the contrary, we should attempt to have a civil conversation with family and friends who fall into this category to help better understand why they are quick to accept what is proven false. We should be demonizing the individuals and organized groups who spread false misinformation to advance whatever agenda is behind their lies. As for those who become victims of these vermin, arguing with them is not the answer; reasoning is. It's worth a try.

May the truth be with you. Beam me up, Scotty.

A call to action. What can we do to avoid being conned? The best way to avoid becoming a victim of untrue information is to be wary of what we read on social media and what we hear on news sources and podcasts. Question both the content and the platforms the info is coming from. Be aware of how _algorithms_ can manipulate what we see and hear. Finally, research beyond the headlines and, by all means, engage common sense. It's really that easy.

The **Consequences** of conspiracy theories and misinformation.

>*False and misleading political information.

*Conspiracy theories and disinformation have fostered distrust in our election system.

*Disinformation fuels distrust and even violent acts.

*Can and has caused much controversy among family members.

*Scammers are everywhere on the Internet, our phones, and our email looking to fleece the unsuspecting. In today's fast-moving, digital information world, question everything.

*Conspiracy theories and misinformation can negatively influence how we vote in elections.

*Misinformation negatively affects adults and children, and it can be dangerous. Many teens, for example, refused to be vaccinated based on false claims they've seen and read on social media.

The final word goes to Carl Sagan.

AMERICA

"At the heart of science is an essential balance between two seemingly contradictory attitudes —an openness to new ideas, no matter how bizarre or counterintuitive they may be, and the most ruthless skeptical scrutiny of all ideas, old and new. This is how deep truths are winnowed from deep nonsense."

—*Carl Sagan*—
(1934 – 1996)
Astronomer, planetary scientist, cosmologist, astrophysicist, astrobiologist, author, & Science communicator

Technology & Social Media

"Technology gives us power, but it does not and cannot tell us how to use that power. Thanks to technology, we can instantly communicate across the world, but it still doesn't help us know what to say."

—Jonathan Sacks—
(1948 – 2020)
British Orthodox rabbi & leading philosopher, theologian & author

What went wrong, and what went right.

Technology advances society in many positive ways, but it cannot and will not save us. Technology is not a living, breathing thing; it's just a tool like any other. It depends on how we use it to our advantage to enhance our lives and not become slaves to it.

In the past 30 years, technology has

AMERICA

added significant advancements in all areas of human life in essential areas such as medicine. NASA technology advances space exploration and our personal lives down here on Mother Earth. That's the good stuff.

Then there are the goodies that Silicone Valley has brought us, some good, some not so good. We now live in the digital world, and if we're not fully engaged in it, guess what? We're simply left behind.

> *"Once a new technology rolls over you, if you're not part of the steamroller, you're part of the road."*
>
> **—Stewart Brand—**
> American author and founder of "The WELL," the "Global Business Network," & the "Long Now Foundation"

Silicon Valley has provided us with a legal addiction called the Smartphone. We use that handy device to shop, pay bills, store information, and even remotely lock or open doors at home. Our phones function as GPS, radio, television, e-reader, and cameras with 5g quality just in case we have ambitions of becoming the next Steven Spielberg, assuming we have a decent screenplay.

STANDING STRONG

We hold our phones in our hot little hands while out walking or jogging, crossing a street, shopping, eating in a restaurant, sitting in a doctor's waiting area, and, yes, in the restroom. We check our text messages, Twitter, Facebook, and Instagram, and how are stocks are doing. And don't you just love it when someone sends a text to several people, and every time one of them replies, your text notification goes off? *Grrrrrrr!!!*

*Brandon Swenson's authored an insightful article in a Grantham University article titled, **Technology: The Good, The Bad, The Ugly** that makes the point, "From communication and time management to manufacturing and healthcare, tech tools have an enormous impact on our lives. There's always a tradeoff, of course, and sometimes it feels like our technology is taking over our lives," Swenson says. "Let's look at the good, the bad, and the ugly sides of technology today—and how we can make sure that we're getting the most out of these tools without falling into some common traps."

The Good. There is no question that we're more connected than ever before, which means that most of our family, friends, coworkers and loved ones are just a text, call, email, or video chat away.

The Bad. Our hyperconnectivity means we may have difficulty disconnecting or creating space to unwind. That can lead to feelings of stress or exhaustion and make it harder to truly relax when we need that rest.

The Ugly. The spread of misinformation or outright lies, the prevalence of bullying and cyberattacks, and other unpleasantries are all common side effects of our cyberspace—and they can lead to anxiety, depression, addiction, and other mental health disorders... Be cautious about what you consume and avoid taking every piece of information you see at face value.

The Balance. As they say, everything in moderation. There are some truly wonderful tools out there, and you don't have to delete your accounts or throw your computer out the window to have a positive relationship with technology. All we need to do is set some reasonable boundaries for ourselves.

*_Brandon Swenson is the communications manager on Grantham University's editorial board. To read the article, Google:_ **Technology: The Good, The Bad, The Ugly**_._

Social media sites have one objective—they're competing for our eyeballs; The more eyeballs, the more advertising revenue. That's why they are in business. And the more data they compile about us, the more they know how to keep our eyeballs on their sites. But, what else do they do with the information they collect? That's a question that a majority of Americans are asking more frequently.

According to **Pew Research**, six-in-ten adults say they do not think it is impossible to go through daily life without having data collected about them by companies or the government. Yet, we readily provide these social media sites with whatever information is requested when we sign up.

A few years back, Facebook thought it would be a great idea to create some new emojis: *thumbs-up, love, ha, ha, wow, sad, and angry.* Facebook's algorithms decided what users would see in their feeds based on which emojis they reacted to more. Guess which one won? More folks responded to "angry" than "likes." We should all be very "angry" at those algorithms that influence what we see and do not on our Facebook pages.

"It has become appallingly obvious that our technology has exceeded our humanity."

—Albert Einstein—
(1878 – 1955)
German-born theoretical physicist

Consider that Mr. Einstein made that statement back when the cool gadgets we have today didn't exist. What would be his reaction if he were here to see how technology has embedded itself in every aspect of our daily routines.

Pew Research Center reports that among the 60% of parents who say their child younger than 12 never uses or interacts with a smartphone, six-in-ten say their child began engaging with the device before the age of 5, including roughly one-third (31%) who say their child began this before age 2 and 29% who say it started between ages 3 and 4. Some 26% of parents whose child uses a smartphone say the smartphone engagement began between the ages of 5 and 8. This share falls to just 14% for parents with a child aged 9 to 11.

That's the ticket; get them hooked young.

<u>To read the report, Google:</u> **<u>Children's engagement with digital devices, screen time</u>**<u>.</u>

Wow, and we thought we had heard it all. Read this wild story from **UK Metro.**

A gorilla named Amare, along with other gorillas, calls the Lincoln Park Zoo in Chicago home. It seems Amare has grown fond of staring at a phone screen. Amare became addicted when zoo-goers began showing him countless pictures and videos on their smartphones through the glass divider of his enclosure. Amare was hooked. However, it became a problem. Amare was paying more attention to the smartphones than the other gorillas in his group. The zoo staff put up a rope to keep people back from the glass partition.

'We are growing increasingly concerned that too much of his time is taken up looking through people's photos; we really prefer that he spend much more time with his troop mates learning to be a gorilla,' Stephen Ross, the director of the zoo's Lester E. Fisher Center for the Study and Conservation of Apes, told the Chicago-Sun Times.

That's one smartphone of a gorilla, but what does it say about what smartphones may be doing to us?

In his article for **Metro**, psychologist Jeff Parson writes, "The debate has been raging for a while now about our device addiction – fueled by unlimited scrolling and endless notification. And a new study has suggested that smartphone addiction physically changes the shape of a human brain similarly to drug addiction."

Jeff Parson is an American psychologist, researcher, educator, and distinguished Professor of Psychology at Hunter College and The Graduate Center of the City

AMERICA

<u>University of New York. To read the article, Google:</u> **<u>Smartphone addiction physically changes the human brain, argue scientists</u>**<u>.</u>

As we said, Silicon Valley has provided us with a legal addiction.

> *"Social media has taken over in America to such an extreme that to get my own kids to look back a week in their history is a miracle, let alone 100 years."*
>
> **—Steven Spielberg—**
> American film director, producer & screenwriter

What is yet to be understood entirely is what all this technology is doing to us? Spoiler alert: You're not going to like the answer.

PsychologyToday.com looked into what technology, specifically our smartphones, is doing to have our faces inches away from the screen all day. In a study, 94% of participants reported feeling troubled when they didn't have their phone, 80% felt jealous when someone else held their phone, and 70% expected to feel depressed, panicked, and helpless if their phone was lost or stolen.

STANDING STRONG

In previous years, the National Human Trafficking Hotline documented nearly 1,000 cases of potential victims of sex trafficking on sites like Facebook, Instagram, and Snapchat.

Make of that what you will.

> *"Everyone's like sheep on social media; like, one person starts making noise, and everyone's like, 'Hey, yeah!' and then you got a whole bunch of People making noise at you."*
>
> **—Earl Sweatshirt—**
> American rapper, songwriter & record producer

And then there are those security cameras. They're attached to buildings, light posts, and doorways. Many are loaded with the latest face recognition capabilities that law enforcement tells us helps catch the bad guys.

The ALCU suggests that the one problem with creating such a robust surveillance system is that it can be abused. The five areas they point to are:

Criminal abuse. Surveillance systems present law enforcement as "bad apples" with a tempting opportunity for criminal misuse.

Institutional abuse. Sometimes, bad policies are set at the top, and an entire law enforcement agency is turned toward abusive ends.

Abuse for personal purposes. Powerful surveillance tools also create temptations to abuse them for personal purposes.

Discriminatory targeting. Video camera systems are operated by humans who bring to the job all their existing prejudices and biases.

Voyeurism. Experts studying how the camera systems in Britain are operated also found that the mostly male (and probably bored) operators frequently use the cameras to spy on women voyeuristically.

Scammers use social media websites and apps to locate their victims. The elderly are often a scammer's target, but the young are being scammed at a higher rate. According to the fraud prevention firm SEON, the data was collected in 2020 by the FBI's Internet Crime

Complaint Center. SEON's "Gen-Z Fraud Report" found those younger than 20 had the most significant year-over-year increase in fraud reports between 2019 and 2020. The 23,186 young people who reported fraud represented a 116% increase from the previous year. Their collective losses totaled about $70.98 million, or about $3,000 per person, in 2020.

Ouch! There is no humor in that.

> *"Technology is a useful servant,*
> *but a dangerous master.*
>
> **—Christian Lous Lange—**
> Norwegian historian, teacher, & political scientist

As they say in those TV ads, *"But wait, there's more,"* The **Metaverse** is coming.

The term 'metaverse' comes from author Neal Town Stephenson's science fiction novel "Snow Crash." The mad techy guys behind the metaverse tell us it will be a new and exciting format to quickly assimilate into our daily lives, work, play, study, and shopping.

Are we not already overwhelmed with what we have?

However, not so fast. The metaverse raises serious questions that need to be asked and answered. Do the major tech companies behind the metaverse create and control the content, and if so, how dangerous is that to us mere mortals? And how will our children be affected by the Metaverse? Will it have a positive or negative effect as they advance into adulthood?

This explanation ***from Taylor & Francis Online*** is just the tip of the iceberg about how we will interact with the Metaverse. "Across the definitions, the common attributes of the metaverse appear to be the continuity (or persistence) of identity and objects, a shared environment, the use of avatars (or embodied self), synchronization, being three-dimensional (or virtual), interoperability, and a user experience that is interactive, immersive, and social. A working definition is an interoperated persistent network of shared virtual environments where people can interact synchronously with other agents and objects through their avatars. This broad and evolving definition can shift as the metaverse continues to be built and used."

To read the article, Google: ***Advertising in the Metaverse: Research Agenda.***

Hmm. Most of us have no idea what this Metaverse is, how it is supposed to enhance or harm our lives, and whether we need another major distraction to add to our time. We can be sure of one thing: one day soon, the Metaverse will descend on us like a thunderstorm.

And here is another problem that David Rothkopf, Professor of International Relations at Johns Hopkins University, was kind enough to point out: "The richest guy on the 2021 Forbes 400 owns the Washington Post. Number 2 now owns Twitter. Number three owns Facebook. Numbers 5 and 6 started Google. Numbers 4 and 9 started Microsoft. Number 10 owns Bloomberg. Free Speech? You decide."

They will control what we see and hear *Nolan Higdon explains in his article on **TheConversation.com**. "During the Gilded Age of the late 19th century and the early 20th century, U.S. captains of industry such as William Randolph Hearst and Jay Gould used their massive wealth to dominate facets of the economy, including the news media. They were, in many ways, prototype oligarchs – by the dictionary definition, "very rich business leaders with a great deal of political influence." Some have argued that the U.S. is in the midst of a Second Gilded Age defined – like the first – by vast wealth inequality, hyper-partisanship, xenophobia, and a new crop of oligarchs using their vast wealth to purchase media and political influence... This consolidation of the media industry in the hands of wealthy individuals is, as media scholar Robert McChesney has argued, especially concerning for a healthy democracy, which necessitates that the electorate has access to an abundance of diverse views and free-flowing information.

Nolan Higdon is a Lecturer of History and Media Studies, California State University, East Bay
To read the article, Google: ***Elon Musk and the oligarchs of the 'Second Gilded Age' can not only sway the public – they can exploit their data, too****.*

Have you heard of **Deepfake** technology? Maybe you've seen something that used it but didn't know it was fake, and a damn good one at that. With AI technology, Deepfakes can take an existing video of anyone and place words in their mouth they never spoke or change someone's face with someone else's. Now apply that to a hotly contested political campaign, for example, where one of the candidates has words put in their mouths that they never actually said, or their terms are slightly changed, and we have a serious problem.

The question of cyber security threats is another challenge that looms like an accident waiting to happen. A foreign country can now reach into our technology and shut down power planets, steal vital government information, and even start wars.

Elon Musk, who looks like he will take over ownership of Twitter, has a few interesting words about the exploding technology of artificial intelligence.

> *"I think we need to be very careful about the advancement of AI... I think the danger of AI is much greater than the danger of nuclear warheads by a lot, and nobody would suggest we allow the world to just build nuclear warheads if they want; that would be insane. And mark my words: AI is far more dangerous than nukes."*
>
> **—*Elon Musk*—**
> Entrepreneur and business magnate

Do Internet providers and governments use this outstanding technology for good, or do we watch it abused by cyber bad guys, AI technology, and algorithms to decide what we will read, watch, share, and believe?

Users beware.

AMERICA

> *"There are a lot of pros and cons about social media; it's just how you choose to handle it and how you have to be prepared for the negatives as well."*
>
> **—*Aubrey Peeples*—**
> The actress known for her role as Layla Grant in the ABC drama series Nashville.

We end this chapter with a prime example of what not to do when exposing our children to technology early. In this case, it was a toddler.

One evening, a young couple entered the restaurant when we were out to dinner. The 30-ish father was carrying a baby girl not old enough to walk. A waitress provided a high chair for the child. The child's father set a glass in front of her and fiddled with his smartphone before placing it against the glass so the child could see it. For the next hour, we watched as neither parent interacted with the child, nor did the child pay them any attention, even when their food arrived. The baby's eyes remained glued to whatever she watched on dad's smartphone.

A sad scene when you picture it.

A Call to Action. What can we do to protect ourselves from fast-moving technology? First, ensure your devices are protected against viruses and spyware. Be conscious of what personal information you share. As new unique technology comes online, the same rules apply. Keep in mind that some companies sell your data whether you want them to. Consider spending less time worrying about your text messages and social media sites. Use the technology to your advantage, not theirs.

The **Consequences** of social media and artificial intelligence abuse.

*Cyberattacks are increasing, affecting thousands of organizations and millions of people daily.
*AI cyberattacks can start wars.
*Social media sites are regularly used to spread misinformation.
*Social media can lead to anxiety, stress, emotional exhaustion, loneliness and depression, misinformation, violation of one's privacy, and dangerous political polarization.
*Social media can lead to low-quality sleep and health

problems.
*Social media can and does affect schoolwork, leading to lower grades.
*Social media is used for cyberbullying and stalking.
*Perhaps the most crucial question is, what does our young's exposure do to social media to them?
*Social media is used to scam older people.
*This list will grow to include new technology.

The last word goes to the late Steve Jobs again.

"Technology is nothing. What's important is that you have faith in people, that they're basically, good and smart, and if you give them the tools, they'll do wonderful things with them.

—Steve Jobs—
(1955 -2011)
Business magnate, industrial designer, investor and media creator & proprietor

STANDING STRONG

AMERICA

Our Government... Emphasis on *"Our"*

"Government is merely a servant – merely a temporary servant; it cannot be its prerogative to determine what is right and what is wrong, and decide who is a patriot and who isn't. Its function is to obey orders, not originate them."

—*Mark Twain*—
(1835 – 1910)
Celebrated author, humorist,
entrepreneur, & lecturer

What went wrong, and what went right.

If America was ever at a crossroads, that time is now. We, the American people, are the only ones that can steer this country in the right direction. Can we put ideology and party loyalty aside long enough to raise our unified voices and let it be known that America is ready for a new era of progress, one that recognizes all citizens equally?

This chapter is not so much a narrative in

the truest sense but highlights some points that not everyone may be familiar with. Read on.

If there is a continuing theme in this book, *We, the People,* are the government. Those we elect to run the government are our employees paid with our tax dollars. Individuals running for public office deserve our respect since we ask them to audition for the job by raising large sums of money to conduct a public campaign for up to a year. Once elected, they become willing employees rewarded with an income of $174,000.00 per year plus a benefits package that most Americans will never achieve.

The dilemma we face is that once we elect them, we move on with our busy lives as if we had no further responsibility. A *"Let George Do it"* mentality takes over. That leads to problems as these employees assume more and more control over our lives because we've abdicated our oversight responsibility. Some wrongfully believe that solving problems with these "employees" means taking matters into their own hands.

On March 4th, 2020, 49-year-old Guy Wesley Reffitt was the first to stand trial for charges in connection with the January 6 breach of the Capital. It took the jury just two hours to find Mr. Reffitt guilty on five charges.

Mr. Refitt had told his family and others that he was fed up with career politicians and a corrupt Congress. He was going to Washington to damn well do something about it. "If they won't follow the laws of the land, we have no reason to follow their laws. Time to remove them." Refitt said. He believed under a "constitutionalist" doctrine, citizens had the authority to disobey any laws they disagreed with.

Whoa! If that were the case, America would be a lawless society.

Mr. Refitt and the others who invaded the Capital to solve "the problem" failed to question why the President of the United States—who took an oath to defend and protect the country—was party to an illegal scheme to keep himself in office.

Millions of Americans will agree with Mr. Reffit on one point: the U.S. Congress requires reform. And yes, too many members of Congress are there too long. On these points, Mr. Reffit has our attention. But where he goes off the rails is his solution on how to fix the problem. Those who committed violent acts on January 6 failed to comprehend how these things are handled in a democracy. First, they are not *"their"* laws; they are *"our"* laws. Second, the constitution calls for the people to participate in free and fair elections, not an armed revolt to overturn the legitimately confirmed election results.

Reffit and his fellow mob members decided that none of that applied to them and proceeded to take matters into their own hands, injuring many Capitol Police and causing some to die. The mob was guilty of not discharging their responsibility as citizens in a civil, passive way. Instead, they listened to wolves in sheep's clothing— *'Latet Anguis in Herba,'* Roman for *'Snakes in the grass'*— who repeatedly lied to them; the invaders had been duped and were on a false mission.

> *"The best government is that which teaches us to govern ourselves."*
>
> **—Johann Wolfgang von Goethe—**
> (1749 – 1832)
> German poet, playwright, novelist, scientist, statesman, theatre director, and critic

In a **Quinnipiac University poll,** a majority of Americans— 58 to 37 percent— think that democracy is in danger of collapse. Just over half of Americans (53 percent) expect political divisions in the country to worsen over their lifetime, 28 percent expect

AMERICA

them to remain about the same, and 15 percent expect them to ease up.

Polls provide a snapshot, but they do not solve problems. People do. As pointed out in the Quinnipiac article, fear of _the enemy within,_ not a foreign threat, punctuates a grim assessment by Americans who believe democracy is in peril caused by a deepening political division.

Whose fault is that?

First, let us agree that it is not _my country;_ it is not _your country;_ it is _our country_. This is not the American Revolution of 1861. Between then and now, we were supposed to get smarter. Some have allowed themselves to fall prey to misleading, deceitful factions who sent them to do their dirty work on January 6.

To read the Quinnipiac poll, Google: **"Quinnipiac National Poll Finds Nearly 6 In 10 Think Nation's Democracy Is in Danger of Collapse_._"**

"Let us not seek the Republican answer or the Democratic answer, but the right answer. Let us not seek to fix the blame for the past. Let us accept our own responsibility for the future."

—John F. Kennedy— (1917 –1963)
35th President of the United States

STANDING STRONG

In his book ***Last Best Hope: America in Crisis and Renewal***, author *George Packer minced no words when he made the critical point that citizens have failed to uphold their end of the democracy bargain. "Self-government is democracy in action – not just rights, laws, and institutions, but what free people do together, the habits and skills that enable us to run our affairs." Packer writes, "**Tocqueville described self-government as an 'art' that needs to be learned. It's what Americans no longer know how to do, or even want to do together. It's hard work, for it needs not just ballots and newspapers and official documents, which we still have, but also trust, which we've lost. It depends on the ability to argue, persuade, and compromise to achieve things for the common good, like the suppression of a catastrophic pandemic. It required you to imagine the experience of others, to recognize their autonomy, and yet to think for yourself."

*From the book **"Last Best Hope: America in Crisis and Renewal"** by George Packer, journalist, novelist, and playwright. **Available at Amazon.com**.*
**Tocqueville was a French aristocrat, diplomat, political scientist & philosopher, and historian.

AMERICA

"Government is instituted for the common good: for the protection, safety and prosperity, and happiness of the people; and not for profit, honor, or private interest of anyone man, family, or class of men.

—John Adams—
(1735 – 1826)
American statesman Founding Father & the second president of the United States

Sorry to have to deliver this message, but there's no blaming anyone else for our problems but ourselves. As wealthy and privileged as any man, Henry Ford reminded us of what can never be overstressed.

"The Government is a servant and never should be anything but a servant. The moment the people become adjuncts to government, then the law of retribution begins to work, for such a relation is unnatural, immoral, and inhuman."

—Henry Ford— (1863 – 1947)
American industrialist, business magnate & Founder of the Ford Motor Company

Mr. Ford's words resonate like ricocheting echoes off the Grand Canyon walls. For the citizens of a democratic nation to sit back and not take personal responsibility to hold those they elect to their oaths of office is a criminal act punishable by... *fill in the rest.*

In the preamble to the Declaration, Thomas Jefferson wisely wrote: "We hold these truths to be self-evident, that all men are created equal, that their Creator endows them with certain unalienable Rights, that among these are Life, Liberty and the pursuit of Happiness-- To secure these rights, Government is instituted among Men, deriving their just powers from the consent of <u>the governed</u> -- That whenever any Form of Government becomes destructive of these ends, it is the <u>*Right of the People*</u> to alter or to abolish it and to institute new Government, laying its foundation on such principles and organizing its powers in such form, as to them shall seem most likely to affect their Safety and Happiness."

The keywording is <u>*to abolish it*</u>, not by an armed and unruly mob invading the United States Capital, but to exercise our responsibility in the voting booth like informed adults where we choose who gets to represent us and who doesn't. If there are problems with anyone we choose, we need only to look inward and question why we repeatedly reelected some of them yet expect a different result.

> *"The will of the people shares the basis of the authority of government; this will shall be expressed in periodic and genuine elections which shall be by universal and equal suffrage and shall be held by secret vote or by equivalent free voting procedures.*
>
> **—*The Carter Center*—**
> Election Standards

One disturbing problem is that we choose candidates based on party affiliation, ideology, or religious beliefs because they think and believe *like us.* That is selfish and self-defeating and leaves us all vulnerable. Elected officials are not there to *mirror us* but to manage the government *for us.* The only common-sense way to judge candidates for public office is by their character, integrity, morals, and qualifications to do the job we ask of them.

Common sense rules.

STANDING STRONG

"I hate all politics. I don't like either political party. One should not belong to them - one should be an individual, standing in the middle. Anyone that belongs to a party stops thinking.

—Ray Bradbury—
(1920 – 2012)
One of the most celebrated 20th-century American writers of fantasy, science fiction, horror, mystery, and realistic fiction

Ask ten people if political parties are affiliated with the government, and six out of ten will say they are or aren't really sure. So much for civics class. Unfortunately, there are no mandatory federal standards for teaching civics or social studies anymore. Instead, each state has its standards that reflect *its priorities and history.* In many school districts, civics is conducted only once, often in a semester-long high school class. There's our problem, folks. We fail to educate our children about how democracy is supposed to work and the role they will play in upholding it as adults.

For the record, political parties are not

affiliated with the government. They're private entities that have morphed into big corporations over these many years with one goal: to maintain control of their product. Spoiler alert: *<u>We, the people, are their product</u>*.

> *In the Soviet Union, capitalism triumphed over communism. In this country, capitalism triumphed over democracy."*
>
> **—*Fran Lebowitz*—**
> American author and public speaker, known for her biting social commentary on American life

Now we come to that dirty little secret: Capitalism. It supports, controls, and influences politics and politicians and, in turn, the decisions politicians make on behalf of their benefactors, corporate America. Capitalism is supposed to work for anyone willing to work hard and succeed, but that is a lie because it doesn't. To expect our elected officials, who benefit directly from corporate America, to correct course is akin to putting our children in charge of the cookie jar.

STANDING STRONG

"We have the best government that money can buy."

—Mark Twain—
(1835 – 1910)
American writer, humorist,
entrepreneur, publisher, and lecturer

"We can either have democracy in this country, or we can have great wealth concentrated in the hands of a few, but we can't have both."

—Louis Brandeis—
(1856 – 1941)
Associate Supreme Court Justice

"Plutocracy is a government controlled exclusively by the wealthy, either directly or indirectly. A plutocracy allows only the wealthy to rule, either openly or by circumstance resulting in policies exclusively designed to assist the wealthy, which is reflected in its name—the Greek words "Ploutos" and "Kratos" translate to wealthy and power or ruling, respectively, in English."

Source: **Investopedia**, Google: **What is a Plutocracy**.

In her newsletter, **"Letters from an**

American," *Historian Heather Cox Richardson wrote: "In the 1850s, 1890s, 1920s, and then again in the modern era, wealthy people had come around to the idea that society worked best if a few wealthy men ran everything. In the 1890s, 1920s, and 2000s, they had gotten there in the same way: first, a popular movement had demanded that the government protect equality of opportunity and equal justice before the law for those who had previously not had either and that popular pressure had significantly expanded rights.

Then, in reaction, wealthier Americans began to argue that the expansion of rights threatened to take away their liberty to run their enterprises as they wished. To tamp down the expansion of rights, they played on the racism of the poorer white male voters who controlled the government, telling them that legislation to protect equal rights was a plan to turn the government over to Black or Brown Americans or immigrants from southern Europe or Asia, who would use their voting power to redistribute wealth.

The idea that poor men of color voting meant socialism resonated with white voters, who turned against the government's protecting equal rights and instead supported a government that favored men of property. As wealth moved upward, popular culture championed economic leaders as true heroes, and lawmakers suppressed voting in order to "redeem" American society from "socialists" who wanted to redistribute wealth. Capital moved upward until a very few people controlled most of it, and then, usually after an economic crash made ordinary Americans turn against the system that favored the wealthy, the cycle began again."

**Heather Cox Richardson is an American historian and professor of history at Boston College. To subscribe to her newsletter, Google: "Letters from an American."*

In ***Democracy of Dollars***, attorney and author, *Richard O. Jacobs wrote what many have yet to understand. "As a society, we have morphed from a Democracy of People into a Democracy of Dollars... consequently, the two political branches of our federal government, the legislative and the executive branches, designed to protect and serve all Americans, have become willing resources to special interests who, in today's pricey politics, can buy their way to the head of the line."

Richard O. Jacobs is an attorney, author, and environmentalist. **"Democracy of Dollars" is available on **Amazon.com**.*

Brookings Institute scholar Darrell M.

West echoes Mr. Jacobs's sentiments when commenting on the new information magnates. "The issue is we are now very dependent on the personal whims of rich people, and there are very few checks and balances on them. They could lead us in a liberal, conservative or libertarian direction, and there is very little we can do about that."

It simply comes down to this: If special interests can buy their way to the head of the line, where does that leave us? Money begets power, and as money and power go, so goes the country.

Forbes reports that American billionaires' financial influence in politics has increased dramatically in the past few campaign cycles. The small, influential group of America's wealthiest now account for nearly 10% of all federal campaign spending—a number that was below 1% before the 2010 Supreme Court decision in Citizens United v. Federal Elections Commission struck down spending limits for corporations and labor unions, opening the floodgates for significant outside spending in federal elections.

Billionaire campaign spending reached a high in 2016, according to the report from **The Institute for Policy Studies** and the liberal group **Americans for Tax Fairness**, contributing over $684 million—more than 41 times higher than the $16.6 million billionaires collectively given in the 2008 election. The report placed the blame squarely on the 2010 <u>*Citizens United Supreme Court decision*</u>, which allowed for the creation of Super PACs and political action committees that operate outside of standard campaigns and without spending limits, as the direct reason for the increase in billionaire spending came down on the side of money, not people.

Make of that what you will.

<u>*To read the report, Google:*</u> **<u>Billionaires Spent 41 Times More On 2016 Election Compared To 2008</u>**<u>.</u>

There may be some hope on the horizon. Congressman Adam Schiff of California has introduced a constitutional amendment to overturn the Supreme Court's *Citizens United* decision and allow for reasonable restrictions on corporate campaign contributions and other spending. We'll see how that goes and how soon, if at all.

> *"It is to be regretted that the rich and powerful too often bend the acts of government to their own selfish purposes."*
>
> **—*Andrew Jackson*—**
> (1767 – 1845)
> 7th President of the United States

AMERICA

Many good and honorable men and women who get elected to Congress go to Washington with the best of intentions. Once there, the Washington two-step system kicks in, and they are often obligated to vote party line, not their conscience. Second, they're required to spend an excessive amount of time each week fundraising for their next election and the party's general fund. They may lose out on plum committee assignments if they don't play by the rules. The system voids an individual's ethics and morality, ensuring those who have neither remain in control.

"One of the penalties for refusing to participate in politics is that you end up being governed by your inferiors."

—*Plato*—

His birth and death occurred in Athens, Greece.
Founded the Platonist school of Thought & Academy, the first institution of higher learning in the Western world.

A***Pew Research Center** report indicates that sixty-four percent of adults (Nearly two-thirds) say they question whether what they hear from elected officials is true and what is not, 16% admit that finding the truth on social media is a challenge, 41% say the same about cable news outlets, and 69% say it is easier to determine the truth when talking with people they know. But even that is challenged by 30% who remain unsure of what they hear when speaking to people they know.

Re-read the *Conspiracy and Misinformation* chapter.

<u>*To read the Pew Research Center report, Google:</u> **<u>Americans' struggles with truth, accuracy, and accountability</u>.**

By its very nature, the government is obligated to reform itself from time to time to reflect our changing society. Who gets to initiate that reform? Why, it's Congress, of course. However, be assured they will first consider how any reform will affect the status quo that keeps theirs, big business, and the power brokers' engines running. And that's no hyperbole.

Thomas Jefferson so eloquently said: "I know no safe depository of the ultimate powers of the society but the people themselves; and if we think them not enlightened enough to exercise their control with a wholesome discretion, the remedy is not to take it from them, but to inform their discretion by *education*. This is the true corrective of abuses of constitutional power."

"America's real moral crisis has nothing to do with people deciding to end their pregnancies, or consenting adults choosing to use contraceptives, or trans young people choosing one bathroom or sports team over another. It has to do with the actions of people in boardrooms and legislative cloakrooms, and the failures of so many who occupy positions of power and public trust to honor the public good."

—*Robert Reich*—
Economist, professor, author, lawyer, and political commentator. Former United States Secretary of Labor

In the 2020 election, despite a record turnout, 80 million eligible voters failed to show up and vote. The idea that 80 million voters chose not to express their voice is a national disgrace.

A National Public Television poll asked people why they failed to vote. Twenty-nine percent were not registered to vote (29%), not being interested in politics (23%), not liking the candidates (20%), a feeling their vote wouldn't have made a difference (16%), being undecided on whom to vote for (10%).

The survey further stated that some said they feel alienated and apathetic, are generally detached from the news, and are pessimistic about politics. A majority believed it made no difference who was elected president, that things would go on just as they always did. Nonvoters were 29 points more likely to say that than people who voted. How do we explain to them how wrong they are, that none of these excuses hold up, that to not cast their votes, they have no voice, and their opinion—which they are quick to share—had no standing.

How do we make eligible voters who failed to vote to understand how wrong they are, that to not vote, they have no voice, and their opinions—which many are quick to share—have no standing. They enjoy the advantages of democracy but are not participants but observers who give nothing back.

There are no free rides in a democracy.

To read the report, Google: ***Despite Record Turnout, 80 million Americans Didn't Vote. Here's Why.***

In ***Democracy of Dollars***, *Richard O. Jacobs wrote: "... As long as the percentage of people voting remains low, neither Congress nor our political parties represent the people's will, nor truly speak for the people... who will speak for the people?... we must. We can no longer be the silent people. Without a concerned, knowledgeable, and active people, today's Democracy of Dollars will continue to prevail, and we will never again be a Democracy of People. We must, as Thoreau put it, become roosters crowing for change."

<u>*Mr. Jacobs and his wife Joan started the Public Interest Law Clinic for Democracy and the Environment at Stetson University College of Law: Google:</u> **Stetson Law to Establish the Dick and Joan Jacobs Public Interest Law Clinic.**</u>

"What is called 'apathy' is, I believe, a feeling of helplessness on the part of the ordinary citizen, a feeling of impotence in the face of enormous power. It's not that people are apathetic; they do care about what is going on but don't know what to do about it, so they do nothing and appear to be indifferent."

—*Howard Zinn*—

(1922 – 2010)
Historian, playwright, philosopher, socialist thinker. Chair of history & social sciences Spelman College – Professor Boston University

Feeling impotent in the face of power is not an excuse for not voting. It's an excuse not to show up and participate and allows the following quote from Alan Greenspan to be self-fulling.

> *"Crony capitalism is essentially a condition in which public officials are giving favors to people in the private sector in payment of political favors."*
>
> ***—Alan Greenspan—***
> American economist & former chair of
> the Federal Reserve in the United States

Never forget the words of the former president when addressing a group of friends during dinner at his Florida Mar-a-Lago estate following the significant tax cut in 2017: "Guys, I just made you all a lot richer."

Make of that what you will.

AMERICA

"The tax relief that this Congress has given now in terms of four tax cuts have overwhelmingly gone to the people at the very top of the income scale in America."

—*Richard Neal*—
U.S. Representative Richard Neal serves the 1st District of Massachusetts

In his book, **"Wild Land: The Making of America's Fury,"** Evan Osnos wrote, "As the sums of money continued to rise, most elected officials in Washington reacted to the distortions of money in politics with versions of 'thoughts and prayers,' a ritual expression of concern, and little else... No politicians are even talking about it... That was because nobody with real power was racing to alter a system that undergirded their positions."

The people with "real power" Mr. Osnos refers to are the citizens of the United States.

<u>From the book **"Wild Land: The Making of America's Fury"** by Evan Osnos, staff writer at The New Yorker and a CNN contributor and a senior fellow at the Brooking Institute, and the 2014 National Book Award winner. His book is available at **Amazon.com.**</u>

STANDING STRONG

"Congress is best viewed from a distance...the farther, the better... because up close, it is truly ugly. I saw most of Congress as uncivil, incompetent at fulfilling their basic constitutional responsibilities (such as timely appropriations), micro-managerial, parochial, Hypocritical, egotistical, thin-skinned, and prone to put itself and re-election before country."

—*Robert M. Gates*—

Intelligence analyst and university president – United States secretary of defense under President George Bush and Barack Obama

Mr. Gates's observations confirm why few well-intentioned qualified people are willing to put themselves and their families through the pernicious political ringer. Who can blame them? Curbing the rise of current political polarization is like trying to herd a bunch of cats. The in-fighting, sniping, hypocrisy, and outright verbal insults between elected officials are shameful, outrageous, and unacceptable. And we wonder why we make little or no progress.

AMERICA

"I think it will take people, true patriots, on both sides of the aisle to say 'enough of this nonsense, we should work together for the good of the people of the United States."

—Ruth Bader Ginsburg—
(1933 – 2020)
Justice of the Supreme Court of the
United States

Times are changing, and just maybe—*maybe*—all is not lost. Generation Z and Millennials are raising their voices and are demanding to be heard. The crumbs we are leaving behind have their attention. They know what is going on in the hallowed halls of the Washington establishment. They see the political posturing, how the wealthy elite has far too much control over our government and their lives, and they're looking to do something about it.

A national poll of Americans, 18 to 29-year-year-olds from the ***Institute of Politics at Harvard Kennedy School,*** showed that most young Americans believe that the world outside our borders is in trouble, but our democracy is in danger also.

"Right now, young Americans are confronting worries on many fronts. Concerns about our collective future—with

STANDING STRONG

regard to democracy, climate change, and mental health—also feel very personal," said 23-year-old Jing-Jing Shen, Student Chair of the Harvard Public Opinion Project. "Yet, amidst all of this uncertainty, and especially coming out of the isolation imposed by the pandemic, young people have come to even more deeply value their communities and connection with others, not only in contending with these crises but also in striving for a meaningful life."

We're counting you, kids; go for it. We may disapprove of your choice of what passes for music these days, but we look forward to hearing your voices and running into you at the voting stations. The future is yours. Handle with care.

<u>To read the poll, Goggle:</u> **<u>Harvard Youth Poll finds young Americans are worried about democracy and even fearful of civil war.</u>**

> *"In framing a government which is to be administered by men over men, the great difficulty lies in this: you must first enable the government to control the governed; and in the next place, oblige it to control itself."*
> **—*James Madison*—**
> (1751 – 1836)
> 4th President of the United States

AMERICA

If you were still around, Mr. Madison, you would see that some have interpreted the Constitution and other enshrined documents as ways to shore up their hold on power. Those who have the gold, as the saying goes, get to rule. The time is now to rewrite that rule.

> *"We can have democracy in this country, or we can have great wealth concentrated in the hands of a few, but we can't have both."*
>
> **—Louis D. Brandeis—**
> (1856 – 1941)
> American lawyer and associate justice on the Supreme Court of the United States

Corporations and their greed for more and more profits are in control of the American Dream, and that's a fact. Just ask the average American family struggling to keep up in a system that does not include them. Read these numbers and weep. They are going in the wrong direction, not for the elite, but for the rest of us. The effective federal corporate income tax rate: 1950-50%—1960-

STANDING STRONG

37%—1970-32%—1980-20%—1990-25% — 2000: 20%—2010-15%—2020: 13%. The federal minimum wage from 2009 – 2022 is $7.25 per hour. Over 60% of Americans live paycheck to paycheck.

Make of that what you will

President James Madison, 4th President of the United States, sent us a warning when he wrote: "Wherever the real power in a government lies, there is the danger of oppression."

Oppression is a strong word. How about we settle for manipulation that will not end until we citizens fulfill our civic duty on behalf of ourselves, our families, our grandkids, and all generation to follow. If we do not, we allow those with the gold to double down to ensure that the status quo remains.

"Our founders recognized that men were not angels and that checks and balances in government were critical to avoid threats to the rule of law."

—*Neal Katyal*—
American lawyer and academic. Former Acting Solicitor General of the United States

AMERICA

Few are aware that back in 1787 in Philadelphia, in the City of Brotherly Love, delegates assembled to complete what would be the infrastructure of the new American government. Any mention of political parties was missing from the document because political parties were viewed as venal remnants of the British monarchical system. The Founders wanted no part of them in favor of a de facto democratic government.

"It was not that they didn't think of parties," said Willard Sterne Randall, professor emeritus of history at Champlain College and biographer of six founding fathers. "Just the idea of a party brought back some bitter memories."

Were you intrigued enough to do a bit of homework?

To read the article, Google: ***The Founding Fathers Feared Political Factions Would Tear the Nation Apart.***

A Call to action. How are we citizens responsible, and what can we do to make our government work better for everyone?

> *First, re-read this chapter. Then take the stance that service in government, particularly in

Congress, is an honor, not a career. There must have term limits.

*The Electoral College no longer reflects the People's will: institute a popular vote and allow ranked-choice voting to ensure free and fair elections.

*Demand an immediate end to all forms of voter suppression and gerrymandering.

*Demand campaign finance reform. The Citizens United ruling must be overturned.

*Close the revolving door between politics and the lobbying industry.

*Members of Congress must be equally responsible under all laws passed that apply to citizens with no exceptions.

*The amount of time candidates' campaign is long and expensive and needs to be shortened.

*All groups engaged in political spending—nationally or on the state level—must disclose their donors. The solution is small donor public financing to put the power back in the hands of individuals.

> *Inside stock trading and a proven immoral act should be cause for dismissal.
> *Coordination between super PACs and candidates must stop. Congress should stop the flow of dark money to nonprofit groups controlled by and promote elected officials.
> *Demand that voter rights are just that; _our rights_ and laws to protect our rights must be passed, and laws restricting voting rights must be challenged.

The **Consequences** of remaining an observer rather than a participant.

> *Political apathy leads to low voter turnout and stagnation.
> *It allows the status quo to remain just that.
> *Lack of voter participation leads to corruption and dishonesty among politicians if they are not held accountable.
> *Political apathy can lead to a loss of democracy.
> *Voter apathy places the power in the hands of the elected.

America's first President, George

STANDING STRONG

Washington, gets the final word. His predictions could not be more appropriate at this moment in time in America.

> *"Political parties are likely in the course of time and things, to become potent engines, by which cunning, ambitious, and unprincipled men will be enabled to subvert the power of the people and to usurp for themselves the reins of government, destroying afterward, the very engines which have lifted them to unjust dominion."*

—*George Washington*—
(1732 – 1799)
1st President of the United States

The Constitution & American Democracy

> *"I agree to this Constitution with all its faults.... I believe, further, that this is likely to be well administered for a course of years, and can only end in despotism, as other forms have done before it when the people shall be so as to need a despotic government, being incapable of any other."*
>
> **—Benjamin Franklin—**
> (1706 -1790)
> Writer, scientist, inventor, statesman, diplomat, printer, publisher, and political philosopher

What went right and what went wrong.

The Founding Fathers created a free and democratic country, but some warned of the evils that could invade the government over time. They had experienced it when under the thumb of British Rule. It was dangerous to have one person—the British King—with too much authority or control. They wanted to warn future generations of our new country of that danger.

At the age of 81, Benjamin Franklin gave his final speech before the Constitutional Convention: "...when you assemble a number of men to have the advantage of their joint wisdom, you inevitably assemble with those men, all their prejudices, their passions, their errors of opinion, their local interests, and their selfish views." He thought it impossible to expect a "perfect production" from such a gathering. Still, he believed that the Constitution they had just drafted, "with all its faults," was better than any alternative that was likely to emerge.

Upon exiting the Constitutional Convention, Franklin was approached by several citizens, asking what sort of government the delegates had created. His answer was: "A republic if you can keep it."

Mr. Franklin's response was clear: democratic republics are not merely founded upon the people's consent. They are also absolutely dependent upon the active and informed involvement of the people for their continued good health.

If there is a lesson to be learned, our Constitution is neither a self-actuating nor a self-correcting document. It requires the constant attention and devotion of all citizens.

Source: National Constitution Center from an article by Dr. Richard Beeman, professor of history and dean of the College of Arts and Sciences at the University of Pennsylvania. Google: ***Perspectives on the Constitution: A Republic, If You Can Keep it.***

"Our new Constitution is now established, everything seems to promise it will be durable; but, in this world, nothing is certain except death and taxes."

—Benjamin Franklin—
(1706 -1790)

On January 6, 1941, President Franklin D. Roosevelt spoke these words at the State of the Union Address to a nation that would soon find itself engaged in World War Two. The theme of his speech was "The Four Freedoms." Today, his encouraging words still have a special meaning.

"The Nation takes great satisfaction and much strength from the things done to make its people conscious of their individual stake in preserving democratic life in America. Those things have toughened the fiber of our people, renewed their faith, and strengthened their devotion to the institutions we make ready to protect. Certainly, this is no time for any of us to stop thinking about the social and economic problems which are the root cause of the social revolution, which is today a leading factor in the world. There is nothing mysterious about the foundations of a healthy and strong democracy. The basic things expected by our people of their political and economic systems are simple. They are Equality of opportunity for youth and others; Jobs for those who can work; Security for those who need it; The ending of special privilege for the few; The preservation of civil liberties for all; the enjoyment of the fruits of scientific progress in a wider and constantly rising standard of living. These are the simple, basic things that must never be lost sight of in our modern world's turmoil and unbelievable complexity. The inner and abiding strength of our economic and political systems depends on how they fulfill these expectations. If the Congress maintains these principles, the voters will give you their applause, putting patriotism ahead of pocketbooks."

Mr. Roosevelt spoke of the benefits democracy offers. Have we, over time, taken it for granted, abused it, and ignored our responsibility to it?

AMERICA

In a speech a few years back, a more current President, Barak Obama, reaffirmed why democracy has survived for as long as it has. "That's who we are. That's our birthright – the capacity to shape our own destiny. That drove patriots to choose revolution over tyranny and our GIs to liberate a continent. It gave women the courage to reach for the ballot, marchers to cross a bridge in Selma, and workers to organize and fight for collective bargaining and better wages. American complacency about political involvement might be chalked up to ignorance of the blood, sweat, and tears shed to win every right. It is largely on social studies teachers to make sure that story is told and understood. It is a story of passionate belief in an idea found in three powerful words that open the Constitution— *We the People.*"

> *"Democracy is worth dying for because it's the most deeply honorable form of government ever devised by man."*
>
> **—Ronald Reagan—**
> (1911 – 2004)
> 40th President of the United States of America

And yet, if Democracy is to work as intended, specific rules apply.

> *"At its roots, Democracy is based upon diversity of thought – political biodiversity. Authoritarian government is based upon uncompromising singular thought. Democracy is based on compromising thought diversity. We are fast moving to authoritarian government."*
>
> **—Robert Reich—**
> Former Secretary of Labor & Chair of Common Cause

Not to beat this subject to the ground, but it may be one of the most important in our lives and should not be treated lightly.

Although we can differ on any number of issues, Democracy should not be one of them. Democracy ensures that we are free to speak our minds and express different ideas. However, democracy demands that we remain firm and unified as a country to ensure that democracy endures. If our unification is currently fractured, those who mislead us, the wolves in sheep's clothing, would let democracy slip away without a second thought to achieve their greedy, ambitious goals that do not align with America's. These wolves instilled public fear and lies that split us, which led to the political slaughterhouse of January 6th.

In his December 2021 article in ***The Atlantic Magazine***, author *Barton Gellman's frightening opening line referred to what occurred on January 6, 2021. "Technically, the next attempt to overthrow a national election may not qualify as a coup. It will rely on subversion more than violence, although each will have its place. If the plot succeeds, the ballots cast by American voters will not decide the presidency in 2024. Thousands of votes will be thrown away, or millions, to produce the required effect. The winner will be declared the loser; the loser will be certified, president-elect."

*Barton Gellman is a critically honored author and journalist, staff writer at **The Atlantic**, and senior fellow at the Century Foundation in New York. To read the article, Google: **Trump's next coup has already begun.**

If left unchallenged, election laws now being passed in some states could turn Mr. Gellman's warning into a reality.

STANDING STRONG

"How little do my countrymen know what precious blessings they are in possession of and which no other people on earth enjoy!"

—*Thomas Jefferson*—
(1743 – 1826)
3rd President of the United States

In an interview, Harry Rubenstein, curator of the National Museum of American History, said, "Democracy means everybody can participate. It means you are sharing power with people you don't know, don't understand, might not even like... that's the bargain. And some people over time have felt very threatened by that notion."

The people Mr. Rubenstein refers to in the last line are those who would strip us of what we have built to achieve all these many years. Power, just behind great wealth, is the ultimate aphrodisiac, and some will go to great lengths to achieve it.

AMERICA

"The death of democracy is now typically administered in a thousand cuts. In one country after another, elected leaders have gradually attacked the deep tissues of democracy—the independence of the courts, the business community, the media, civil society, universities, and sensitive state institutions like the civil service, the intelligence agencies, and the police."

—*Larry Jay Diamond*—
Considered one of the world's foremost scholars on democracy

It is difficult to fathom why an appalling 80 million eligible voters failed to do so in the 2020 election. Did those non-voting-citizen contribute to a Stockholm-based **International Institute for Democracy** report that stated, for the first time, that The United States finds itself added to a list of "backsliding democracies? The report stated, "The United States, the bastion of global democracy, fell victim to authoritarian tendencies itself and was knocked down a significant number of steps on the democratic scale," the 2021 report concluded.

It is not a distinction we should be proud of.

STANDING STRONG

Richard O. Jacobs, author of **Democracy of Dollars,** wrote, "What is going on is not a joke, nor something we can ignore. Nor is it someone else's problem. It is my problem. It is your problem. It's our problem. I know most of us don't like to play the game of politics. But there won't be a democracy or a game of politics if the looming 'slow-moving coup' reaches fruition. A democracy cannot survive as a one-party system. Only despotic corruption does. Venezuela, Egypt, and the Philippines are run by despots who were first democratically elected. Then carelessly ignored by the people as the despots solidified power."

> *"In this time of testing, will we do our duty? Will we do what we must? Will we defend our Constitution? Will we stand for truth? Will we put duty to our oath above partisan politics? Or will we look away from the danger, ignore the threat, embrace the lies and enable the liar? There is no gray area when it comes to that question. When it comes to this moment, there is no middle ground."*

—*Elizabeth Lynne Cheney*—
United States Representative from Wy.

AMERICA

A call to action. Why are we at fault, and what can we do about it? We cannot afford to be observers but participants if we hope to protect what we have. Education is the answer. Know the candidates and the issues well enough to vote and have your vote count. It is our country, our very freedom, that is at stake. Only we can protect it against an unthinkable future under tyranny. It's that simple.

The **consequences** of the possible demise of American Democracy. The excerpts in this chapter clearly show the implications are obvious and do not need not be repeated here. If democracy does not stand, the American democratic way of life will be stripped from future generations. Is that our legacy to the future men and women of America?

In the chapter title, ***Who Are We Anyway?*** We included a quote from Mahatma Gandhi. It is repeated here.

STANDING STRONG

"No man's life can be encompassed in one telling. There is no way to give each year its allotted weight, to include each event, each person who helped to shape a lifetime. What can be done is to be faithful in spirit to the record and try to find one's way to the heart of the man."

—*Mahatma Gandhi*—
(1869 – 1948)

Mahatma Gandhi devoted his adult life to fighting for India's independence from British rule. "My ambition is no less than to convert the British people through non-violence and thus make them see the wrong they have done to India," Gandhi said.

Although India finally won its independence, Gandhi's hope for a unified country did not prevail. The final plan partitioned the subcontinent along religious lines—Hindu India and Muslim Pakistan. India had gained its independence, but religious hatred between the Muslims and the Hindus persisted.

On January 30, 1948, 78-year-old Gandhi was shot to death by Hindu extremist Nathuram Godse. He was angry at Gandhi's tolerance of Muslims. This violent act by one fanatic took the life of a pacifist who spent his life preaching peace through nonviolence. Yes, India won the fight for its independence but lost the war because of the ongoing hatred of the two internal factions—an essential lesson to remember.

On December 7, 2021, in a ceremony to commemorate the attack on Pearl Harbor, an aging military veteran who was there on December 7, 1941, spoke of the true meaning of democracy. When asked by a reporter what the war meant to him, he answered: "When I take walks around my hometown, people often greet me and thank me for my service. I tell them... *You were worth serving for.*"

The final word goes to Thurgood Marshall.

"Where you see wrong or inequality or injustice, speak out, because this is your country. This is your democracy. Make it. Protect it. Pass it on."

—*Thurgood Marshall*—
(1908 – 1993)
Associate Justice of the Supreme Court of the United States

Closing Salvo

In the year it took to assemble this book, the events covered were evolving from day to day, requiring constant updates. At times it felt like completing a thousand-piece puzzle with many tabs missing. As facts continue to unravel, only then can we begin to evaluate what we have learned. Where we go from here remains an open question.

As I wrote in the *Introduction*, there is a storm on the horizon, and this time it feels dangerous. This time we may be on a crash course of historic proportions. American democracy or autocracy? What do the American people want? We are entering a dark period in American history as we try to make sense of it all.

Consider that not one of the many conspiracy theories has proven to be accurate, nor has the endless flow of misinformation, which has been fact-checked repeatedly. If we hope to implement workable solutions, the madness must stop, and common sense must be our guide. Divisiveness weakens us; unity makes us strong.

AMERICA

The words of Warren G. Harding, the 29th President of the United States, bear repeating: "America's present need is not heroics, but healing; not nostrums, but normalcy... The country does not require a revolution, but restoration; not agitation, but adjustment; not surgery, but serenity; not the dramatic, but the dispassionate; not experiment, but equipoise."

"We have this one life to appreciate the universe's grand design, and for that, I am extremely grateful."

—*Stephen Hawking*—
(1942 – 2018)
Theoretical Physicist

With Mr. Hawking's words etched in our memory, we are left to wonder; if we could spend a few moments gazing down from the void of space at our home, what would we see, and how might it change us as it did Neil Armstrong?

This is not by any means the end of our story; this isn't even the beginning of the end. There will always be new challenges requiring new and workable solutions. Until then, sit back in your favorite chair, turn on

YouTube.com, and listen to Israel Kamakawiwo' ole's inspiring version of ***"Somewhere Over the Rainbow."*** Then listen to Neil Diamond singing ***"America."***

"What we call the beginning is often the end. And to make an end is to make a beginning. The end is where we start from."

—*T.S. Elliot*—
(1888 -1965)
Thomas Stearns Eliot was a poet, essayist, publisher, playwright, literary critic, and editor & one of the 20th century's major poets

Lessons I Learned

Richard O. Jacobs

One Earth, but One World?...

February 27, 2022. This blog was first published in 2016. A few weeks ago, I spoke to Stetson University College of Law Students about the lessons I learned over the nine decades I've been privileged to be on this earth. During the Q&A, a frustrated student raised a question about the contentious environment we live in today. My answer included, "If today's attitude among us prevailed during World War II [when I was in junior high school] we never would have won the war." The insensitive, politicized, unsupportive comments of our politicians today, particularly those of our former president and his supporters, following Russia's invasion of Ukraine, which in ways parallels Germany's invasion of Czechoslovakia at the start of WW II, brought this message to the fore.

I'M NOT SURE WHY I REMEMBER THE

STANDING STRONG

ELECTION OF 1940 – I was only nine years old. But I do. Maybe it was because my dad lost his business in the early 1930s, not long after the depression began, then pulled himself out of the morass and rebuilt his business; then, despite his gutsy effort, he lost it again in the collapse of 1938. My parents' mindset: a political change was desperately needed, one favorable to business.

But the depression wasn't the only thing troubling American minds in 1940.

During the late thirties and as the forties began, life was chaotic, beyond the depression that wouldn't go away.

Hitler's deadly Panzers were thundering through Western Europe.

And a fierce debate was building in America between isolationists, perhaps the American majority, who wanted no part of the war, and interventionists, who said it was time – despite our economic depression – for us to get involved, not only to help England and what was left of Western Europe but to ensure our own survival. Franklin Delano Roosevelt, running for his third term as the Democratic presidential candidate, was an interventionist, championing building war-readiness and foreign aid to England, a country staggering from bombardment by the Nazi war machine.

AMERICA

That year, the Republican convention was held in Philadelphia.

Isolationists Thomas E. Dewey, the favorite, and Robert A. Taft dominated the early going for the Republican nomination. Dewey, then Taft, led early rounds, but neither produced enough votes for nomination. As the German blitzkrieg picked up speed, the convention became more chaotic and contentious – worse than in 2016 – as the influence of the interventionists grew. After five indecisive ballots, support for the isolationists faded, and the Republicans nominated the dark-horse candidate Wendell Willkie, a nonparticipant in all of the primaries.

Once a Democrat, Willkie, a rising-star lawyer, and businessman, had joined the Republican Party and sought the presidency because he believed Roosevelt's policies were anti-business (the point my struggling parents supported). Like recent Republican presidential candidates, Romney and Trump, Willkie's credentials were those of a successful CEO.

Willkie's early campaign focused on America's domestic issues, but as the European war escalated, though still leaning toward isolation, his focus shifted. He vowed to keep American troops out of the war; however, during the campaign, Willkie and

STANDING STRONG

Roosevelt communicated frequently about America's foreign aid programs, and Willkie became openly supportive. Fortunately, foreign aid to England and Western Europe never became a campaign issue. (In later years, historians wrote that Willkie's support of Roosevelt's war-aid programs probably saved England and ultimately the outcome of World War II.)

Roosevelt won the 1940 election. Willkie garnered but 45% of the popular vote.

THEN, SOMETHING SPECIAL HAPPENED.

On January 19, 1941, the day before he was sworn in for his third term, Roosevelt asked Willkie for his help. He asked Willkie to go to England as his representative – to confirm America's support. What better, more uniting, message could there be than a message of America's support and unity conveyed by the leader of the opposition party at the request of the President?

By such a simple insight and act, both seemingly impossible in today's contentious political reality game, *political combatants became partners*!

Susan Dunn wrote in the New York Times:

"As the war crisis deepened, F.D.R. and Willkie became almost a team. 'The leader of the Republican party himself — Mr. Wendell

Willkie — in word and in action, is showing what patriotic Americans mean by rising above partisanship and rallying to the common cause,' Roosevelt would say in a speech in March 1941."

Willkie's trip to England was followed by his testimony before Congress supporting Roosevelt's lend-lease programs, which was followed by more missions as Roosevelt's representative: China, Russia, and the Middle East. Willkie's October 1942 radio report to the American people about his journey around the world and talks with our allies was heard by 36 million Americans. He opened Americans to "connectedness" to the idea that – as there is but one earth – there also is but one world, and all of us are its inhabitants and its responsible members. Historian Samuel Zipp wrote:

"Willkie enchanted them with the story of his encounter with the people of the world, from a Baghdad shopkeeper and a Soviet factory superintendent to Charles De Gaulle, the Shah of Iran, Joseph Stalin, and Madame Chiang Kai-shek, while also challenging readers to embrace the new spirit of global connection and interdependence he claimed to have discovered everywhere he went."

Willkie's radio report was followed by his book, *One World*, that quickly sold millions of copies. Zipp concludes:

STANDING STRONG

"Willkie's book capitalized on a new yet widely shared sense that technology and war had made the world small — and potentially interdependent — but it brought that reality home in a felt as much as intellectual manner. [Zipp then quotes Robert van Gelder, NY Times book reviewer]: 'We all know what has happened to distance in these last years. But between the knowing and the feeling, between the knowledge and the emotional understanding, there is almost inevitably a gap. Willkie's book is like a spark that closes that gap.'"

Willkie's One World (1943)

Sometime in the distant past – I think in my late teens or early 20s – I read Willkie's *One World*. After our 2016 political convention, I pulled my tattered copy off the shelf and reread it. Willkie frames his "one-world" conclusions in his Introduction:

"These convictions are not merely humanitarian hopes; they are not just idealistic and vague. They are based on things I have learned at first hand and upon the views of men and women, important and anonymous, whose heroism and sacrifices give meaning and life to their beliefs."

In a chapter titled "Our Imperialisms at Home," he writes:

"Freedom is an indivisible word. If we

want to enjoy it and fight for it, we must be prepared to extend it to everyone, whether they are rich or poor, whether they agree with us or not, no matter what their race or the color of their skin.... [W]whatever we take away from the liberties of those whom we hate, we are opening the way to loss of liberty for those we love."

In his last chapter, appropriately titled "One World," Willkie describes the futility that followed the First World War:

"We entered into an era of strictest detachment from world affairs. Most of our public leaders, Democratic and Republican, went about the country proclaiming ... that never again should we allow ourselves to become entangled in world politics.... We shut ourselves away from world trade.... We sacrificed a magnificent opportunity for leadership.... The responsibility for this does not attach solely to any political party."

He also writes about the negative effect of rammed-through party politics:

"President Wilson negotiated the peace proposals at Versailles, including the covenant of the League, without consultation with or participation of the Republican leadership in the Senate. He monopolized the issue for the Democratic party and thereby strategically caused many Republicans – even international-minded Republicans – to take the

opposite position."

WILLKIES' FINAL WARNING:
*"The time is approaching when we must once more determine whether America will assume its proper position in world affairs, and **we must not let that determination be again decided by mere party strategy**."*

I doubt we will ever assume our "proper position in world affairs" until we control our tribalism – and its resulting polarized party strategy. Yes, we have one earth; now, we must learn to see our earth as one world – the only home for all of life on earth. That is our challenge.

As we ponder the lessons we might gain from Willkie's hands-on experiences, which broadened his worldview, something I wrote in Chapter 7 of *Wonderlust* might be helpful:

"[C]consider the possibility that our Creator didn't shape the DNA of some of us to be conservative in our political or philosophic thinking because being conservative is always rational and right, and all people should be conservative. Nor did our Creator shape the DNA of others among us to be liberal in our political or philosophic thinking because being liberal is always rational and right, and all people should be liberal. Our globe is

populated by people with differing points of views and insights for a reason. We gain from lessons provided to us through the wisdom of each other. If we have the sensitivity to listen to and consider those whose ideas don't fit comfortably within our own mind's frames, we will make better decisions. That's why today's political polarization is so sad and so nonproductive."

Richard O. Jacobs, Attorney, Author, Climate Activist – author of Democracy of Dollars.
<u>*Mr. Jacobs's book "Democracy of Dollars" is available on Amazon.com*</u>

The Eastman Memo

John Eastman, a conservative lawyer working with then-President Donald Trump's legal team, presented a two-page memo that he believed to be a legal argument to overturn the 2020 election. They would attempt to persuade then-Vice President Mike Pence to ignore the Constitution and toss out the 2020 election results on January 6 and install then president Trump for another four years. The document, reprinted here in its entirety, became known as "The Eastman Memo."

**PRIVILEGED AND CONFIDENTIAL
January 6 scenario**

Seven states have transmitted dual slates of electors to the President of the Senate.

The 12th Amendment merely provides that "the President of the Senate shall, in the presence of the Senate and House of Representatives, open all the certificates and the votes shall then be counted." There is very solid legal authority and historical precedent for the view that the President of the Senate does the counting, including the resolution of disputed electoral votes (as Adams and Jefferson did while Vice President, regarding their own election as President), and all the members of Congress can do is watch.

The Electoral Count Act, which is likely unconstitutional, provides: If more than one return or paper purporting to be a return from a State shall have been received by the President of the Senate, those votes, and those only, shall be counted which shall have been regularly given by the electors who are shown by the determination mentioned in section 5 of this title to have been appointed, if the determination in said section provided for shall have been made, or by such successors or substitutes, in case of a vacancy in the board of electors so ascertained, as have been appointed to fill such vacancy in the mode provided by the laws of the State; but in case there shall arise the question which of two or more of such State authorities determining what electors have been appointed, as mentioned in section 5 of this title, is the lawful tribunal of such State, the votes regularly given of those electors, and those only, of such State shall be counted whose title as electors the two Houses, acting separately, shall concurrently decide is supported by the decision of such

State so authorized by its law; and in such case of more than one return or paper purporting to be a return from a State, if there shall have been no such determination of the question in the State aforesaid, then those votes, and those only, shall be counted which the two Houses shall concurrently decide were cast by lawful electors appointed in accordance with the laws of the State, unless the two Houses, acting separately, shall concurrently decide such votes not to be the lawful votes of the legally appointed electors of such State. But if the two Houses shall disagree in respect of the counting of such votes, then, and in that case, the votes of the electors whose appointment shall have been certified by the executive of the State, under the seal thereof, shall be counted.

This is the piece that we believe is unconstitutional. It allows the two houses "acting separately" to decide the question, whereas the 12th Amendment provides only for a joint session. And if there is disagreement, under the Act, the slate certified by the "executive" of the state is to be counted, regardless of the evidence that exists regarding the election and regardless of whether there was ever a fair review of what happened in the election, by judges and/or state legislatures.

So, here's the scenario we propose:

1. VP Pence, presiding over the joint session (or Senate Pro Tempore Grassley, if Pence recuses himself), begins to open and count the ballots, starting with Alabama (without conceding that the procedure, specified by the Electoral Count Act, of going through the States alphabetically is required).

2. When he gets to Arizona, he announces that he has multiple slates of electors and so is going to defer a decision on that until finishing the other States. This would be the first break with the procedure set out in the Act.

3. At the end, he announces that because of the ongoing disputes in the 7 States, there are no electors that can be deemed validly appointed in those States. That means the total number of "electors appointed" – the language of the 12th Amendment -- is 454. This reading of the 12th Amendment has also been advanced by Harvard Law Professor Laurence Tribe (here).

A "majority of the electors appointed" would therefore be 228. There are at this point 232 votes for Trump and 222 votes for Biden. Pence then gavels President Trump as re-elected.

4. Howls, of course, from the Democrats, who now claim, contrary to Tribe's prior position, that 270 is required. So, Pence says, fine. Pursuant to the 12th Amendment, no candidate has achieved the necessary majority. That sends the matter to the House, where the "the votes shall be taken by states, the representation from each state having one vote..." Republicans currently control 26 of the state delegations, the bare majority is needed to win that vote. President Trump is re-elected there as well.

5. One last piece. Assuming the Electoral Count Act process is followed and, upon getting the objections to the Arizona slates, the two houses break into their separate chambers, we should not allow the Electoral Count Act

constraint on debate to control. That would mean that a prior legislature was determining the rules of the present one — a constitutional no-no (as Tribe has forcefully argued). So, someone – Ted Cruz, Rand Paul, etc. – should demand normal rules (which includes the filibuster). That creates a stalemate that would give the state legislatures more time to weigh in to formally support the alternate slate of electors if they had not already done so.

6. The main thing here is that Pence should do this without asking for permission – either from a vote of the joint session or from the Court. Let the other side challenge his actions in court, where Tribe (who in 2001 conceded the President of the Senate might be in charge of counting the votes) and others who would press a lawsuit would have their past position -- that these are non-justiciable political questions – thrown back at them, to get the lawsuit dismissed. The fact is that the Constitution

assigns this power to the Vice President as the ultimate arbiter. We should take all of our actions with that in mind.

Author's note: Needless to say, this was debunked. As Dan McLaughlin wrote in the National Review: "Taken as a whole, Eastman's memo reeks of the kind of advice you give a client when you start with the conclusions and have to backfill your way through a long series of insurmountable obstacles."

The executive order to seize voting machines

December 16, 2020

PRESIDENTIAL FINDINGS
TO PRESERVE, COLLECT AND ANALYZE
NATIONAL SECURITY INFORMATION
REGARDING THE 2020 GENERAL ELECTION

By the authority vested in me as President of the United States pursuant to the Constitution and laws of the United States of America, including Article 2 section 1 of the U.S. Constitution, Executive Orders 12333,

AMERICA

13848, National Security Presidential Memoranda 13 and 21, the International Emergency Economic Powers Act (50 U.S.C. 1701 et seq.) (IEEPA) and all applicable Executive Orders derived therefrom, the National Emergencies Act (50 U.S.C.1601 et seq.) (NBA), and section 301 of title 3, United States Code:

I, Donald J. Trump, President of the United States, find that the forensic report of the Antrim County, Michigan voting machines, released December 13, 2020, and other evidence submitted to me in support of this order, provide probable cause sufficient to require action under the authorities cited above because of evidence of international and foreign interference in the November 3, 2020, election. Dominion Voting Systems and related companies are owned or heavily controlled and influenced by foreign agents, countries, and interests. The forensic report prepared by experts found that "the Dominion Voting System is intentionally and purposefully designed with inherent errors to create systemic fraud and influence election results. The system intentionally generates an enormously high number of ballot errors. The intentional errors lead to bulk adjudication of ballots with no oversight, no transparency, and no audit trail. This leads to voter or election fraud." The report found the election management system to be wrought with unacceptable and unlawful vulnerabilities—including access to the Internet—probable cause to find evidence of fraud, and numerous malicious actions.

There is also probable cause to find that Dominion Voting Systems, Smartmatic, Electronic Systems & Software, Hart Inter Civic, Clarity Election Night Reporting, Edison Research, Sequoia, Scytl, and similar or related entities, agents, or assigns, have the same flaws and were subject to foreign interference in the 2020 election in the United States. There is probable cause to find these systems bear the same crucial code "features" and defects that allowed the same outside and foreign interference in our election, in which there is probable cause to find votes were in fact altered and manipulated contrary to the will of the voters. Dominion Voting Systems is based in Toronto, Canada, and assigns its intellectual property including patents on its firmware and software to Hong Kong and Shanghai Bank Corporation (HSBC), a bank with its foundation in China and its current headquarters in London, United Kingdom.

The Dominion Voting system is owned and

controlled by foreign entities. Multiple expert witnesses and cyber experts identified acts of foreign interference in the election prior to November 3, 2020, and continued in the following weeks. In fact, there is probable cause to find a massive cyber-attack by foreign interests on our crucial national infrastructure surrounding our election—not the least of which was the hacking of the voter registration system by Iran. (B.O. 13800 of May 11. 2017)

Just days prior to the election of November 3, 2020, federal Judge Totenberg found, after three days of testimony, including by Dominion executive Eric Coomers:

> There are "true risks posed by the new BMD [Ballot Marking Device of Georgia's Dominion Voting Systems] voting system as well as its manner implementation.
>
> These risks are neither hypothetical nor remote under the current circumstances. The insularity of the Defendants' and Dominion's stance here in the evaluation and management of the security and vulnerability of

the BMD system does not benefit the public or citizens' confident exercise of the franchise. The stealth vote alteration or operational interference risks posed by malware that can be effectively invisible to detection, whether intentionally seeded or not, are high once implanted, if equipment and software systems are not properly protected, implemented, and audited. The modality of the BMD systems' capacity to deprive voters of their cast votes without burden, long wait times, and insecurity regarding how their votes are actually cast and recorded in the unverified QR code makes the potential constitutional deprivation less transparently visible as well, at least until any portions of the system implode because of a system breach, breakdown, or crashes. Any operational shortcuts now in setting up or running election equipment or software create other risks that can adversely impact the voting process.

AMERICA

"The Plaintiffs' national cybersecurity experts convincingly present evidence that this is not a question of "right this actually ever happen?" - but *when it will happen, especially if further protective measures are not taken. Given the masking nature of malware and the current systems described here, if the State and Dominion simply stand by and say, "we have never seen it." the future does not bode well.

"Still, this is year one for Georgia in implementation of this new BMD system as the first state in the nation to embrace statewide implementation of this QR barcode-based BMD system for its entire population. Electoral dysfunction - cyber or otherwise - should not be desired as a mode of proof. It may well land, unfortunately, on the State's doorstep. The Court certainly hopes not." [FOOTNOTE 1: Case 1:17-cv-02989-AT Document 964 Filed 10/11/20 Page 146 of 147]

And, yet it did. Every defect and hazard of which Judge Totenberg warned happened in Georgia. Witnesses in Georgia have provided evidence of crashes, the replacement of a server, impermissible updates to the system, and connections to the Internet, and both Coffee and Ware counties have identified a significant percentage of votes being wrongly allocated contrary to the will of the voter. Coffee County Georgia has refused to certify its result.

Accordingly, I hereby order:

> (1) Effective immediately, the Secretary of Defense shall seize, collect, retain and analyze all machines, equipment, electronically stored information, and material records required for retention under United States Code Title 42, Sections 1974-1974(e), including but not limited to those identified in footnote 1. The Secretary of Defense has discretion to determine the interdiction of national critical infrastructure supporting federal elections. Designated locations will be identified in the operation order.

AMERICA

(2) Within 7 days of commencement of operations, the initial assessment must be provided to the Office of the Director of National Intelligence. The final assessment must be provided to the Office of the Director of National Intelligence no later than 60 days from commencement of operations.

(3) The Director of National Intelligence shall deliver this assessment and appropriate supporting information to the President, the Secretary of State, the Secretary of the Treasury, the Secretary of Defense, the Attorney General, and the Secretary of Homeland Security.

(4) A direct liaison to be authorized to coordinate as required between the applicable U.S. Departments and Agencies.

(5) The Secretary of Defense may select by name or by unit federalization of appropriate National Guard support.

(6) The Assistant Secretary of Defense for Homeland Security

will coordinate support requirements as needed from the Department of Homeland Security.

(7) The appointment of a Special Counsel to oversee this operation and institute all criminal and civil proceedings as appropriate based on the evidence collected and provided all resources necessary t carry out her duties consistent with federal laws and the Constitution.

DONALD J. TRUMP, PRESIDENT OF THE UNITED

Acknowledgments

Thanks to Stan and Sally Pots, Jennie Rosenblum, JoAnn Lilla, Charlie Bregg, and my wife Susanne for reading an early draft and providing valuable feedback. To Richard O. Jacobs for his friendship and insight into all things human. To Lisa Orban, Publisher of Indies United Publishing House, for her patients, support, and expertise. And to all those whose excerpts represent the voices of truth, facts, and reason that are the heart of this book. Lastly, to all those quoted, past and present, for sharing their knowledge and wisdom.

ABOUT THE AUTHOR

ROBERT J. EMERY

WRITER-PRODUCER-DIRECTOR-AUTHOR

Email: media8@verizon.net
website: www.robertjemeryauthor.com
Facebook:
https://www.facebook.com/rjemery/
Twitter: @bobemery

**Current member of:
The Directors Guild of America**
The Alliance of Independent Authors

Other books by Robert J. Emery under the pen name R.J. Eastwood
Midnight Black, a suspense/thriller Novel
The Autopsy of Planet Earth, a science fiction adventure

Over his four-decade career, Robert J.

Emery has written, produced, and directed projects ranging from local and national television commercials, corporate communications films, writing and directing feature motion pictures, and network television documentaries.

Mr. Emery's interest in production and all things entertainment began in the Air Force branch of Armed Forces Radio and Television. Upon his discharge, he became an on-air personality and news reporter at WCLW Radio in Mansfield, Ohio. Upon moving to Canton, Ohio, Mr. Emery opened an advertising agency, which led to writing and directing local TV commercials. He created and directed a daily one-hour morning TV talk show hosted by former Miss USA Diana Batts and TV personality Carl Day. In 1965 he wrote and directed his first feature film, *The Bittersweet Night, followed by Willy & Scratch, Dare the Devil, Scream Bloody Murder, Sign of Aquarius, Ride in a Pink Car, The Florida Connection,* and his last, *Swimming Upstream* for the Lifetime Television Movie Channel. That film was awarded the *Sapphire Halo Award for Best Dramatic Motion Picture* at the Los Angeles Angel City Film Festival.

As writer, producer, and director, Mr. Emery's television productions include the MSNBC primetime documentary *"For God & Country; A Marine Snipers story,"* hosted by NBC's Lester Holt. The program won the

National Headliner Award for Best Documentary or Series of Reports and the Special Jury Award in the informational category of the Professional News Division (CINE Golden Eagle Competitions). He created the Starz/Encore series, The Directors, which also ran in re-run on the Reels Channel and in over 75 countries worldwide. *The Directors* won the Silver Plaque Award in the *2002 Chicago International Television Competition and the Award of Excellence 2003 Accolade Awards.* The episode featuring George Lucas won First Place at Florida Motion Picture & Television Association Awards for best television series episode. *That was followed by the four-hour PBS mini-series* **The Genocide Factor,** hosted by Academy Award© winner Jon Voight. The production won the *Houston International Worldfest Gold Special Jury Award for Best Television & Cable TV Series/Documentary.* He produced and directed *KidHealth,"* a 13-episode PBS series on children's healthcare in America hosted by Olympic Gold Medalist Peggy Fleming. Produced and directed **Golden Saddles, Silver Spurs,** and the history of Western Cinema for Starz/Encore Western Channel.

For his numerous productions for Shriners Hospital for Children, Mr. Emery received top honors for nine years at the New York Film Festival.

In 2006 Mr. Emery retired from active

production and began work on his first novel, *In the Realm of Eden,* published in January 2010. The novel was selected as one of the top five finalists by the *Next Generation Indie Book Awards Competition.* Mr. Emery is the author of four non-fiction books based on his television series, *The Directors.* His two other novels are the science fiction thriller *The Autopsy of Planet Earth* and the suspense thriller *Midnight Black,* which together garnered him nine book awards.

Mr. Emery was born and raised in Bristol, Rhode Island. He currently resides with his wife in Florida. When not writing or working on a project around the house, Mr. Emery spends time in the kitchen fixing great Italian meals thanks to the teachings of his Italian mother and the delight of his wife, children, grandchildren, and friends.

www.ingramcontent.com/pod-product-compliance
Lightning Source LLC
Chambersburg PA
CBHW071952070526
44583CB00015B/1164